Paranormal phenomena

Paranormal Phenomena

Other Books of Related Interest:

Opposing Viewpoints Series

Alternative Medicine

Current Controversies Series

Medical Ethics

At Issue Series

Life and Death

"Congress shall make no law ... abridging the freedom of speech, or of the press."

First Amendment to the U.S. Constitution

The basic foundation of our democracy is the First Amendment guarantee of freedom of expression. The Opposing Viewpoints Series is dedicated to the concept of this basic freedom and the idea that it is more important to practice it than to enshrine it.

OPPOSING
VIEWPOINTS®
SERIES

Paranormal Phenomena

Karen Miller, Book Editor

GREENHAVEN PRESS
A part of Gale, Cengage Learning

GALE
CENGAGE Learning™

Detroit • New York • San Francisco • New Haven, Conn • Waterville, Maine • London

GALE
CENGAGE Learning™

Christine Nasso, *Publisher*
Elizabeth Des Chenes, *Managing Editor*

© 2008 Greenhaven Press, a part of Gale, Cengage Learning.

Gale and Greenhaven Press are registered trademarks used herein under license.

For more information, contact:
Greenhaven Press
27500 Drake Rd.
Farmington Hills, MI 48331-3535
Or you can visit our Internet site at gale.cengage.com

For product information and technology assistance, contact us at

Gale Customer Support, 1-800-877-4253
For permission to use material from this text or product, submit all requests online at www.cengage.com/permissions

Further permissions questions can be emailed to permissionrequest@cengage.com

Articles in Greenhaven Press anthologies are often edited for length to meet page requirements. In addition, original titles of these works are changed to clearly present the main thesis and to explicitly indicate the author's opinion. Every effort is made to ensure that Greenhaven Press accurately reflects the original intent of the authors. Every effort has been made to trace the owners of copyrighted material.

Cover photograph reproduced by permission of Barnaby Hall/Riser/Getty Images.

LIBRARY OF CONGRESS CATALOGING-IN-PUBLICATION DATA

Paranormal phenomena / Karen Miller, book editor.
   p. cm. -- (Opposing viewpoints)
  Includes bibliographical references and index.
  ISBN-13: 978-0-7377-4008-0 (hardcover)
  ISBN-13: 978-0-7377-4009-7 (pbk.)
  1. Parapsychology. I. Miller, Karen, 1973-
  BF1031.P3317 2008
  130--dc22

                                              2008000817

Printed in the United States of America
1 2 3 4 5 6 7 12 11 10 09 08

Contents

Chapter 1: Why Do People Believe in Paranormal Phenomena?

Chapter 2: Do Paranormal Phenomena Exist?

Chapter 3: Are the Mind and Body Separate Entities?

Chapter 4: Should Government Support the Paranormal?

Why Consider Opposing Viewpoints?

> *"The only way in which a human being can make some approach to knowing the whole of a subject is by hearing what can be said about it by persons of every variety of opinion and studying all modes in which it can be looked at by every character of mind. No wise man ever acquired his wisdom in any mode but this."*
>
> *John Stuart Mill*

In our media-intensive culture it is not difficult to find differing opinions. Thousands of newspapers and magazines and dozens of radio and television talk shows resound with differing points of view. The difficulty lies in deciding which opinion to agree with and which "experts" seem the most credible. The more inundated we become with differing opinions and claims, the more essential it is to hone critical reading and thinking skills to evaluate these ideas. Opposing Viewpoints books address this problem directly by presenting stimulating debates that can be used to enhance and teach these skills. The varied opinions contained in each book examine many different aspects of a single issue. While examining these conveniently edited opposing views, readers can develop critical thinking skills such as the ability to compare and contrast authors' credibility, facts, argumentation styles, use of persuasive techniques, and other stylistic tools. In short, the Opposing Viewpoints Series is an ideal way to attain the higher-level thinking and reading skills so essential in a culture of diverse and contradictory opinions.

In addition to providing a tool for critical thinking, Opposing Viewpoints books challenge readers to question their own strongly held opinions and assumptions. Most people form their opinions on the basis of upbringing, peer pressure, and personal, cultural, or professional bias. By reading carefully balanced opposing views, readers must directly confront new ideas as well as the opinions of those with whom they disagree. This is not to simplistically argue that everyone who reads opposing views will—or should—change his or her opinion. Instead, the series enhances readers' understanding of their own views by encouraging confrontation with opposing ideas. Careful examination of others' views can lead to the readers' understanding of the logical inconsistencies in their own opinions, perspective on why they hold an opinion, and the consideration of the possibility that their opinion requires further evaluation.

Evaluating Other Opinions

To ensure that this type of examination occurs, Opposing Viewpoints books present all types of opinions. Prominent spokespeople on different sides of each issue as well as well-known professionals from many disciplines challenge the reader. An additional goal of the series is to provide a forum for other, less known, or even unpopular viewpoints. The opinion of an ordinary person who has had to make the decision to cut off life support from a terminally ill relative, for example, may be just as valuable and provide just as much insight as a medical ethicist's professional opinion. The editors have two additional purposes in including these less known views. One, the editors encourage readers to respect others' opinions—even when not enhanced by professional credibility. It is only by reading or listening to and objectively evaluating others' ideas that one can determine whether they are worthy of consideration. Two, the inclusion of such viewpoints encourages the important critical thinking skill of objectively evaluating an author's credentials and bias. This evaluation will illuminate an author's reasons for taking a particular stance on an issue and will aid in readers' evaluation of the author's ideas.

It is our hope that these books will give readers a deeper understanding of the issues debated and an appreciation of the complexity of even seemingly simple issues when good and honest people disagree. This awareness is particularly important in a democratic society such as ours in which people enter into public debate to determine the common good. Those with whom one disagrees should not be regarded as enemies but rather as people whose views deserve careful examination and may shed light on one's own.

Thomas Jefferson once said that "difference of opinion leads to inquiry, and inquiry to truth." Jefferson, a broadly educated man, argued that "if a nation expects to be ignorant and free ... it expects what never was and never will be." As individuals and as a nation, it is imperative that we consider the opinions of others and examine them with skill and discernment. The Opposing Viewpoints Series is intended to help readers achieve this goal.

David L. Bender and Bruno Leone,
Founders

Introduction

Carl Sagan was an astronomer who made outer space famous. The host of the popular *Cosmos* television series, he was a respected researcher who had a gift for capturing the imagination of the general public for all the wonders and possibilities that space exploration held for the future of mankind—far beyond the "simple" marvel of walking on the moon. He made science interesting, and not just because his awe and enthusiasm about it were contagious. He proposed outrageous and exciting things. He believed, openly, that there was intelligent life rampant in the universe. Aliens were everywhere. What he did not believe, however, was that they had come to visit: The physical space of the galaxy, much less the universe, is too vast. The longevity of intelligent species is unknown, especially compared to how much time had passed since the creating of the universe. There are no artifacts to reasonably suggest that extraterrestrial beings had visited our planet. As eager as Sagan was to believe that ETs (extraterrestrials) were just around the galactic corner, logic and evidence presented to him a much more compelling case that they were far beyond our reach even if they actually were out there. He publicly engaged in wishing, but he did not engage in wishful thinking.

In some ways, Sagan represents both skeptics of and believers in paranormal phenomena. He believed in proof and in possibility. This frame of mind is currently reflected by a large portion of American society, especially regarding the paranormal. Professional skeptics like Michael Shermer and James Randi share the field with professional paranormalists like the medium John Edward and the spoon-bending Uri Geller. In between the two camps sit just about everyone else: people who do not spend much time or resources officially investigating the paranormal, and who make their decisions according to what seems plausible.

Despite all the hand-wringing from skeptics and academics about the gullible public and complaints from proponents of the paranormal about the pervasive cynicism and lack of faith in modern times, Americans as a group have taken a thoughtful interest in the paranormal debate. Western culture is interested in the fantastic possibilities that paranormal phenomena promise, but it wants to understand paranormal phenomena as something more substantial than magic. Rather than conducting discourse in town hall meetings or in journals and newspapers, the subject is discussed in the entertainment industry. Television programs and movies mirror both extremes of the paranormal argument, as well as the general ambivalence toward paranormal phenomena.

Medium is a television crime-solving drama based on real-life psychic detective Allison DuBois. *Crossing Over* is a reality television series in which the host John Edward passes messages from the spirit world to members of the audience. These two programs present paranormal phenomena as natural and legitimate without suggesting in any way that such a viewpoint is controversial. In opposition to this stance are programs like *Penn & Teller: Bullsh*t!*, an investigative series produced by magicians Penn Jillette and Teller (who goes by only his last name) that unreservedly attempts to expose paranormal phenomena and practitioners as misled or false. Still, the bulk of the programs addressing the paranormal phenomena debate tackle the middle ground. *Heroes* and *The 4400* are both classed as science fiction, not fantasy; they portray characters who suddenly find themselves with extraordinary powers beyond the known laws of physics, such as the ability to fly, heal others, read minds, or create realistic illusions. In each of these storylines, however, are biological and medical reasons that explain these abilities. In *Heroes*, people with abilities represent the human species on the cusp of evolution, with identifying markers in their DNA. In *The 4400*, the abilities result from an injection of a (fictional) neurotransmitter "promicin," which activates an unused part of the brain. In film, Peter Parker becomes Spiderman after being bitten by an irradiated spider. The X-Men are born with genetic mutations. The Fantastic Four develop their superpowers after encountering cosmic energy that mutates their DNA.

In the examples cited above, paranormal ability is just a manifestation of a scientific phenomenon—nothing mysterious about it (except for the fact that the scientific phenomenon has not been discovered in the real world yet)! As Arthur C. Clarke puts it, "Any sufficiently advanced technology is indistinguishable from magic." The average person does not so much believe in the existence of paranormal phenomena as in the idea that reality and possibility are probably just waiting for science to catch up.

Of course, not every purported claim about the paranormal is reasonable, and not every dismissive doubt is founded. In the end, individuals are left to decide for themselves what is true, what is possible, and what is fantasy. As happens with any decision, people turn to the experts for advice and listen to the ones they find most believable. The viewpoints in *Opposing Viewpoints: Paranormal Phenomena* present arguments from both sides of the debate about the existence of the paranormal in the following chapters: Why Do People Believe in Paranormal Phenomena? Do Paranormal Phenomena Exist? Are the Mind and Body Separate Entities? Should Government Support the Paranormal? Ultimately, readers will have to make up their own minds about the existence of paranormal phenomena, either on a case-by-case basis or once and for all.

CHAPTER 1

Why Do People Believe in Paranormal Phenomena?

Chapter Preface

In the book *Why We Believe What We Believe* (2006 Free Press), authors Andrew Newberg and Mark Waldman explore the origins of personal belief systems:

> "In most schools of philosophy, proof is inextricably bound to logic, reason, and personal experience, but . . . personal experience is subject to numerous perceptual, emotional, and cognitive distortions that occur at every stage of neural processing. What is finally summoned forth into consciousness turns out to be a very limited and subjective view of the world."

> "Science tries systematically to utilize subjective experience to measure objective reality, but even scientific views of reality differ. . . . Furthermore, a scientist's belief system can influence the outcome of a study as much as a theologian's belief can influence his or her perception of the world."

The authors make the argument that each person can only know for certain what he or she has experienced. All shared knowledge, therefore, is a form of belief, whether it concerns the physical or the metaphysical world.

For one person to have knowledge is a great thing, but progress happens when people share knowledge and work together. Inspiration may come to an individual, but technological advances are made by a society. Unless many people believe that an idea has merit, it is unlikely to develop further. Innovators who want to implement change, therefore, have a vested interest in knowing why other people believe what they do—so they can propagate those beliefs or change them. Individuals, however, are loath to abandon their beliefs, precisely because they are so personal. According to Newberg and Waldman, many beliefs arise from childhood memories and intense emotional experiences; they are unique to the person who holds them, and are cherished parts of his or her identity not to be given up without compelling reasons.

This matter of belief is particularly relevant to the adversarial field of paranormal investigation. The very definition of "paranormal" excludes scientific explanations for unusual events, so traditional scientists are not likely to find room in their belief systems to even entertain the possibility that paranormal phenomena exist. Investigators gathering evidence to prove the existence of paranormal phenomena take offense at such a dismissal of their work, because they consider themselves to be scientists who are performing rigorous study and are participating in scientific discourse, too. Furthermore, for one side to succeed it must prove the other side wrong.

Not all scientific investigations are "win-lose": one biologist who discovers a medicinal use for a bacteria does not necessarily prove wrong another biologist investigating how that same bacteria survives in a hostile environment. But a paranormal investigator who proves definitively that ESP (extrasensory perception) is real also proves spectacularly wrong any scientists who disagree. On paper, of course, every scientific investigator believes that the discovery of truth benefits humanity, no matter what that truth is. In reality, however, scientific investigators are ordinary people with feelings that can be hurt and careers that can be derailed. The consequences of being proven wrong once and for all affect far more than a theory—they can upset a personal or professional life.

The investigation of paranormal phenomena is thus accompanied by the investigation of paranormal meta-belief: the study of *why* people believe what they do about the existence of paranormal phenomena. If a traditional scientist or paranormal investigator knows how or why people develop prejudices for or against the existence of paranormal phenomena, he or she can use that information to influence the beliefs of an audience about new investigative data. Because people and society are complicated, the pursuit of knowledge is not pristinely noble. Scientists analyze the development of belief so they can teach other people to think as they do; in a sense, they are recruiting teammates to intimidate their opponents by force of numbers. Repeated experimentation with reproducible results may be the only reliable path to new discoveries, but scientists find comfort and encouragement (and sometimes financial backing) in an idea's popularity, too.

The following chapter explores the reasons why people believe in or are skeptical of paranormal phenomena, and of what significance those beliefs are to the advancement of knowledge and the pursuit of truth.

| "*ESP experiments have been replicated and their results are as consistent as many medical trials.*"

Skeptics Ignore Evidence for Paranormal Phenomena

Robert Matthews

Robert Matthews is a visiting reader in science at Aston University in Birmingham, in the United Kingdom. He also writes about science-related issues for a variety of newspapers and magazines and is the author of the book 25 Big Ideas: Science that Is Changing Our World. *Originally trained as a physicist, his interests now lie chiefly in the use and abuse of statistical methods by the scientific community. In the following viewpoint, Matthews analyzes how scientists often debate the results of paranormal experiments, even when data are as significant as the results from experiments in other disciplines, such as medicine.*

As you read, consider the following questions:

1. According to the rules of Bayes's theorem, how is scientific belief similar to predicting horse races?

2. What reasons do skeptics give for ignoring the evidence supporting the existence of extrasensory perception?

3. How does parapsychology research reveal flaws in the scientific method?

So, you think you are rational, dispassionate and swayed only by hard evidence? Then try this little test. Last September [2002] two teams of respected scientists unveiled the outcome of research to prove the effectiveness of two very different agents. One team reported a powerful effect, much larger than expected by chance alone; the other could only muster an indifferent result with borderline significance. Which of these do you find the more convincing proof?

Most of us would view this as a no-brainer, and cite the first. But you probably sense a trap and would like to know more before deciding.

The weak result came from an international team of medical scientists studying a new drug aimed at reducing the chances of recurrent heart attacks. They found that the odds of another heart attack fell by just a few per cent, barely better than the reduction expected by chance alone. The far stronger finding came from a team at the Koestler Parapsychology Unit at the University of Edinburgh, UK, and seems to support the existence of extrasensory perception (ESP).

Still feel happy to put your trust in hard data? Or do you find yourself reaching for all kinds of reasons why, in this case, the experimental results alone just aren't enough to assess the merits of a scientific finding?

If so, you're in good company. For years, well-designed studies carried out by researchers at respected institutions have produced evidence for the reality of ESP. The results are often more impressive than the outcome of clinical drug trials because they show a more pronounced effect and have greater statistical significance. What's more, ESP experiments have been replicated and their results are as consistent as many medical trials—and even more so in some cases. In short, by all the normal rules for assessing scientific evidence, the case for ESP has been made. And yet most scientists still refuse to believe the findings, maintaining that ESP simply does not exist.

Despite this relentless rejection of their work, parapsychologists such as those at the Koestler unit have ploughed on in search of clinching evidence they hope will convince the scientific community. Some believe it is a waste of time because the reality of ESP has now been put beyond reasonable doubt. Sceptics agree it is fruitless, but on the grounds that since ESP cannot exist, all positive results must be spurious. How has such a split arisen? After all, scientific evidence is supposed to drive everyone towards a single view of reality.

Evidence and Belief

Over the years, sociologists and historians have often pointed out the glaring disparity between how science is supposed to work and what really happens. While scientists routinely dismiss these qualms as anecdotal, subjective or plain incomprehensible, the suspicion that there is something wrong with the scientific process itself is well founded. The proof comes from a rigorous mathematical analysis of how evidence alters our belief in a scientific theory. And it is not so easy to write off.

Its starting point is a profound result derived independently by the mathematicians Frank Ramsey and Bruno de Finetti in the 1930s. They showed that you can assign a number to the touchy-feely concept of belief using ideas drawn from probability theory. In particular, they proved that your faith in a theory can be quantified objectively on a scale ranging from near 0 for disbelief to near 1 for certainty. They also showed that scientific reasoning is logical provided your beliefs follow a rule known as Bayes's theorem.

Widely used in probability theory, Bayes's theorem shows how the chances of an event happening change in light of developments, such as the odds of a horse winning a race given that it won its last one. Ramsey and de Finetti showed that exactly the same rule applies to updating belief in a theory as new evidence comes in. The good news is that their rule is very simple: just take your original level of belief and multiply it by the strength of the new evidence, as captured by the so-called likelihood ratio. This gives the relative probabilities of getting such evidence if the theory is true, compared to if it were false. The likelihood ratio is large if the findings are consistent with theory, thereby boosting your level of belief in it.

But there is a nasty surprise lurking in the Ramsey-de Finetti analysis. How do you arrive at that original level of belief? In many scientific studies, there is a wealth of insight and evidence on which people can base their prior level of belief. But in novel or controversial areas of research, such as the paranormal, there isn't. And in those cases, it can only be based on gut feeling, instinct and educated guesses. In other words, it is entirely subjective.

Science Is as Subjective as Objective

This disturbing conclusion seems utterly at odds with the conventional view of science. Every week, research journals publish hard evidence supporting a host of theories, backed by statistical arguments for taking it seriously. Bayes's theorem implies that this whole process is nothing more than an elaborate attempt to dodge the subjectivity at the root of every scientific result.

While this prompts outrage among defenders of the scientific faith, many working scientists acknowledge that subjectivity plays a big role in their day-to-day thinking. Behind closed doors they routinely dismiss claims for, say, some new link between cancer and diet, simply because they find it implausible.

Nor is such prejudice the preserve of the life sciences. Even theoretical physicists routinely resort to subjective arguments to see off awkward results. Hearing that his new theory of

How Drug and ESP Trials Compare

Research into ESP is routinely criticized for producing inconsistent results that show no signs of converging over time. Yet this is a common trait in many scientific studies. The first 10 trials of the blood-clot-dissolving drug streptokinase produced varied results that struggled to achieve statistical significance even when pooled. Yet the lifesaving capabilities of streptokinase are now regarded as a triumph of modern medicine. Recent studies of ESP, in contrast, point to a greater effect and one with more statistical significance.

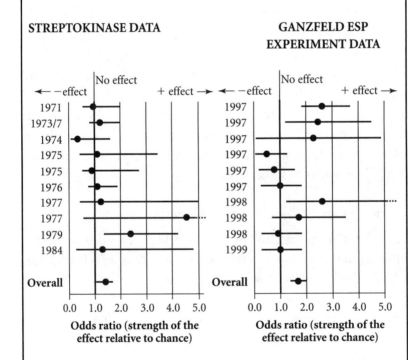

STREPTOKINASE DATA

GANZFELD ESP EXPERIMENT DATA

TAKEN FROM: Robert Mathews, *New Scientist*, 2004.

special relativity had lost out to rival theories in its first experimental test, Albert Einstein simply brushed the evidence aside, arguing that the other theories were less probable.

Whether they realise it or not, scientists' thinking is influenced by Bayesian reasoning, and nowhere is this more apparent than in attitudes towards ESP research. By the standards of conventional science, the weight of evidence is now very impressive, but the scientific community refuses to accept the reality of ESP. Instead, they insist that extraordinary claims demand extraordinary evidence.

Too Many Explanations

This is the perfect example of Bayesian reasoning. But who decides when an "extraordinary" level of evidence has been reached? It is something that can, and clearly does, mean different things to different people. Ultimately, it is not strength of evidence, or lack of it, that has been at the heart of the controversy over ESP. Yet the response of sceptics has been the same: whatever was responsible for the positive findings, it cannot be ESP. Something else must have happened: some flaw in the experiment, say, or a slip-up in the data analysis. Perhaps even fraud.

It is a response that provokes understandable resentment among parapsychologists. They complain that exactly the same approach could be used to reject unwelcome findings in any other field of science. It is too easy, they argue, for critics to dream up endless ways to explain positive ESP findings. Sceptics, meanwhile, insist it is only right to eliminate every alternative explanation before reaching a final conclusion.

Bayes's theorem shows that both camps are right. But it also reveals another disturbing fact: wrangling over alternative explanations can never be ended objectively. The reason is that every attempt to test a scientific theory involves a slew of "auxiliary hypotheses"—assumptions made about the design of experiment, the data analysis, and even the mindset of the researchers. For instance, medics confronted with the results of a clinical trial they find implausible routinely check the researchers' affiliations to see if they have a reason to show the results in a particular light. And perhaps this is justified, given that academic studies funded by industry are more prone to producing positive findings. If the medics do suspect that the research findings are skewed, they will water down their faith in the results no matter how statistically significant they may be.

Skeptics Explain Away Evidence

In the case of ESP research, the mindset of researchers has become a key issue. Some studies suggest believers are more likely to get positive results than sceptics. For sceptics, this is proof of the auxiliary hypothesis that they insist explains all evidence for ESP: slipshod or dishonest practice by true believers hell-bent on proving their case. Others, however, see it as just another case of an intriguing effect that has been observed in many other areas of research.

Even so, it is only after all these alternative explanations have been dismissed that researchers can claim their results have been vindicated. Once again, the Ramsey-de Finetti analysis provides a mathematical rule for deciding when it is safe to say that evidence best matches the theory under test, rather than some auxiliary hypothesis. The bad news is that the rule demands estimates for the plausibility of competing explanations, which is again subjective.

The worst suspicions of parapsychologists are thus entirely justified. It is impossible to find evidence for ESP that will win round the sceptics. But those who see this as final proof of the futility of parapsychology should ponder this: exactly the same holds true for all scientific research. There are always auxiliary hypotheses, and deciding whether the evidence backs them or the theory being tested is just a matter of judgement.

The famous criterion of "falsifiability," the notion that scientific theories can never be proved, only disproved, is therefore a comforting myth. In reality, scientists can (and do) dream up ways to explain away awkward findings. The only difference with parapsychology is that scientists have no qualms about invoking everything from incompetence to grand conspiracy to explain the results.

It therefore seems that all that parapsychologists can do is collect ever more evidence, in the hope of gradually persuading more scientists of the reality of ESP. In this, they are appealing to one of the central tenets of the scientific process: that as more evidence builds up, the case for a theory becomes ever stronger. Yet the mathematics of scientific inference reveals even this to be a myth.

The Likelihood Ratio

Bayes's theorem shows that belief in a theory increases with the strength of evidence. Mathematically, this is captured by the likelihood ratio (LR)—the likelihood of getting such evidence if the theory is true, compared to if it were false. So, for example, if the evidence is 10 times as likely to emerge if the theory is true rather than false, the LR is 10, and belief in the theory increases tenfold. If, however, the evidence is twice as likely to emerge if the theory is false, then the LR is 0.5, and the level of belief is halved.

All of this is perfectly reasonable—except how do you convert raw data into the all-important LR? The answer is, there is no hard and fast rule. It is yet another occasion for judgement, opinion and educated guesswork. Subjectivity has once more reared its head, and this time it undermines the most cherished principle of the scientific process: that, in the end, the accumulation of evidence ensures the truth will come out.

Once again, parapsychology provides an important lesson. Over and over again, reputable researchers have found strong evidence for the existence of ESP in tightly controlled experiments. Many would conclude the evidence is more consistent with the existence of ESP than any other explanation, such as sloppy methodology or fraud. As such, the LR is a large number, and should greatly increase belief in the existence of ESP—or so the parapsychologists would argue.

Sceptics, on the other hand, claim that pretty much any explanation for the evidence is more plausible than ESP, so the LR is far less than 1. So any fresh evidence actually reduces their belief in ESP.

Same Evidence, Different Conclusions

The upshot could hardly be more different from the standard view of the scientific process. Both camps can look at precisely the same raw data and legitimately reach utterly different conclusions, because they have radically different models for the cause of the data. One camp insists that the results are more plausibly caused by ESP than anything else; the other camp simply does not agree.

It gets worse. As the evidence accumulates, the two camps will not only fail to reach consensus but actually be driven further apart—propelled by their different views about the LR. And worst of all, there is no prospect of such a consensus unless the two sides can agree about the cause of the data.

Does the evidence accumulated over all these years prove the existence of ESP? By now, it should be clear that there is no objective answer. It should also be clear this is not the fault of parapsychologists. It simply reflects the fact that science alone cannot give us what we seek: an objective view of reality.

More than any other scientific discipline, parapsychology pushes the scientific process to its limits, and reveals where its faults lie. In particular, it has highlighted that, contrary to the insistence of many scientists, data alone can never settle this or any other issue.

This does not bode well for parapsychologists hoping to amass enough evidence to convince even hardened sceptics of the reality of ESP. It shows instead that there is only one way forward: for both sides of the debate to agree on their models for the results that emerge from ESP experiments. That, in turn, means working together in good faith to devise tests whose outcome can be agreed upon by all. For the key lesson of the mathematics of scientific inference is ultimately very simple: the credibility of all evidence is a matter of trust.

> *"I suspect that telepathy, clairvoyance, psychokinesis, and life after death do not exist because I have been looking in vain for them for twenty-five years."*

Evidence for Paranormal Phenomena Has Not Been Found

Susan Blackmore

Dr. Susan Blackmore is a psychologist and writer whose research on consciousness and anomalous experiences has been published in over sixty academic papers, as well as book chapters, reviews, and popular articles. Her doctorate degree is in parapsychology, and she spent twenty-five years looking hopefully for proof of paranormal phenomena before giving up. In the following viewpoint, Blackmore explains her decision to pursue research in other directions, and postulates why people believe in the paranormal even when they have no evidence to support it. This essay appears in Skeptical Odysseys, *a collection of reflections by skeptical writers and investigators about their involvement in the skeptical movement.*

As you read, consider the following questions:

1. How does the author portray the common perception of skeptics? How does she distinguish her skepticism from that portrait?

2. Why does the author design an experiment to test a product she assumes is worthless?

3. Why do skeptics and believers cling to their beliefs in the face of contrary evidence?

Imagine this ... Imagine a world in which if you love some-one enough, or need them enough, your minds will communicate across the world wherever you are, regardless of space and time. Imagine a world in which, if only you can think a thought clearly and powerfully enough it can take on a life of its own, moving objects and influencing the outcome of events far away. Imagine a world in which each of us has a special inner core—a "real self"—that makes us who we are, that can think and move independently of our coarse physical body, and that ultimately survives death, giving meaning to our otherwise short and pointless lives. This is (roughly speaking) how most people think the world is. It is how I used to think—and even hope—that the world is. I devoted twenty-five years of my life to trying to find out whether it is. Now I have given up.

If any one of these three possibilities turned out to be true then the world is a fundamentally different place from the one we think we know, and much of our science would have to be overthrown. Any scientist who discovered the truth of any of these propositions—or, even better, was able to provide a theory to explain them—would surely go down in the history of science as a hero; as the woman who changed the face of science forever. As Richard Dawkins puts it, "The discoverer of the new energy field that links mind to mind in telepathy, or of the new fundamental force that moves objects without trickery around a tabletop, deserves a Nobel Prize, and would probably get one."

This is something that many critics of skepticism just don't see. I am often accosted by people who seem to think that I think as follows (Note—I don't!): "I am a scientist. I know the truth about the universe from reading my science books. I know that telepathy, clairvoyance, psychokinesis, and life after death are impossible. I don't want to see any evidence that they exist. I am terrified that I might be wrong." The way I really think is more like this: "I am a scientist. I think the way to the truth is by investigation. I suspect that telepathy, clairvoyance, psychokinesis, and life after death do not exist because I have been looking in vain for them for twenty-five years. I have been wrong lots of times before and am not afraid of it." Indeed I might add that finding out that you are wrong, and throwing out your previous theories, can be the best way to new knowledge and a deeper understanding.

I long ago threw out my own previous beliefs in a soul, telepathy, and an astral world, but even then I kept on searching for evidence that my new skepticism was misplaced, and for new theories that might explain the paranormal if it existed. I kept doing experiments and investigating claims of psychic powers. Finally I have given up that too.

One of the reasons I have given up is probably a trivial and selfish one—that I have simply had enough of fighting the same old battles, of endlessly being accused of being scared of the truth or even of trying to suppress the truth; of being told that if I don't come and investigate x (my near-death experience, my psychic twin, Edgar Cayce, the miracle of Lourdes, D.D. Hume, or the haunted pub round the corner) that proves I have a closed mind. It doesn't. It only proves that after years of searching for paranormal phenomena and not finding them, I am no longer prepared to spend my precious time and limited energy in documenting yet another NDE; setting up more carefully desired experiments to test telepathy in twins; going over all the reams of published argument about Cayce, Lourdes, or Hume; or sitting up all night waiting for the ghost that (because I am a psi-inhibitory experimenter) will never come. . . .

Confronting Assumptions

People are not always so willing to grapple with evidence. In 1998 I was reading the only newspaper available on a holiday flight when I saw a photograph of Cherie Blair, the [former British] prime minister's wife, wearing something called a bio-electric shield. Apparently this attractive pendant hanging round her neck reduced her stress and protected her from harmful radiation. [Former First Lady] Hillary Clinton was said to own one too. I was angry. I assumed the pendant had no effect. How could intelligent and high-profile people like this possibly believe in, much less promote, such lies? Then I noticed the price—£119 (US $139) for the cheapest, and £749 (US $995) for the gold version, and was sufficiently angry to want to do something about it.

First, I realized I was jumping to conclusions. What if the shields really did work? If they did then some extraordinary new principle must be involved and I would learn something very exciting indeed. If they did not then the facts should be made known. I decided to do some experiments to find out.

The bioelectric shield Web site and leaflets make several claims, among them that "The shield utilises principles of physics to help you cope with the energy overload/stress of your daily life." Each shield "contains a composition of a matrix of precision-cut quartz and other crystals designed to balance and strengthen your natural energy field." My own favorite is this: "Not only does this crystal force field deflect harmful electromagnetic energies coming from your Computer Screens, Cell Phones, Microwaves, Hair Dryers and other electronic equipment but it deflects any personal energy that is incompatible with you. The shield resonates at your personal frequency after wearing it for 24 hours, it will act as a 'Gatekeeper' letting in only energies that are compatible with you and deflecting those not compatible with you."

These were the claims I had to test, and test fairly. On the positive side the effects were mostly measurable, such as increasing muscular strength, reducing stress, and improving well-being. Among the problems of testing it was that the shield takes some time to balance itself to a person's personal energy and that it cannot be shared with anyone else. This meant doing a long-term study with one shield per person.

Enlisting Bioelectric Shield's Help

I tracked down the British distributor, David Chambers, and through him the American manufacturer, Virginia Brown, and after many discussions they supplied us with six real and six fake shields. Nick Rose and I asked twelve women to wear these for several weeks and measured their hand strength, mood, and stress levels at regular intervals, without either them or us knowing which shields were which. We tried to arrange the double-blind precautions to be fair to both the manufacturers and to us. We did not want to find either that we had negative results and they thought we could have cheated, or positive results and we thought they could have cheated. Arranging this was not easy, partly because they did not seem to understand what was required. Eventually, however, we all agreed that Nick and I would prepare results for each subject coded by letter and a list of who had worn which numbered shield, and that David and Virginia would come to our lab with a list of which of the numbered shields was fake and which real. We would exchange these in front of an independent witness so that neither side could cheat.

Up until the moment they arrived I had been obsessed with the precautions, but as soon as they arrived I knew there was no need. They were genuine, eager to find out the results, and trying to give us their code list even before we got into the lab. We stopped them from doing so and laid out the re-

Caring for Your BioElectric Shield

About once a month, hang your Shield either in a window, or preferably, outdoors, rain or shine, for 6 hours during the day. The energy from the sun will be conducted through the metal to the crystals, recharging them, and keeping them good for decades to come. If you are hanging it in a window that blocks certain parts of the light spectrum, leave it for 8 hours. *Make sure you bring in your shield before the moon rises,* since moon light is reflected sun light, and can draw energy away from your Shield.

If you leave it out overnight, hang your Shield out for twice as many days as it was left in the moonlight. If you want to make sure it's working at maximum efficiency you can send it back to have it re-charged in our crystal room, and repolished.

"Wearing and Caring for Your Shield," 2007
www.bioelectricshield.com.

sults for them. This way they could see, out of twelve subjects, who had become stronger, more relaxed, or calmer, and we gave them the chance to choose, from these twelve people, which six they thought had worn the real shields. By chance they should get three right; with the probability of getting four right 0.24, five 0.04, and six 0.001. In other words, if they correctly chose five or six of the subjects we would have a significant result. We could analyze the complete results later. David and Virginia studied the graphs carefully, made their choice, and then handed over the code list.

It was a genuinely exciting moment. We believed no one could have cheated and we had no idea which shield was which. If they got five or six right we would know we had some strange and incomprehensible effect on our hands. If not we would know we had more false and potentially damaging claims to deal with. We took their list and marked up the graphs. They had gotten four right.

Explaining Away Evidence

What happened next was the most informative event of all. They began to explain what had happened. This person had obviously been blocking the shield's energy. This person may have needed longer with the shield—shields can spend at least four weeks rebalancing some people. This person had become more relaxed even with a fake shield. Over lunch we talked more—they seemed disappointed, but only slightly so. They were sure there was some explanation, and they never seemed to entertain the possibility that the shields do nothing at all.

Later we did the full analysis and sent them the results. Virginia wrote that she had initially thought the results were a disaster but finally came to see them as a "blessing in disguise." Apparently her consultant told her that the placebo shields should not be made by the same person as the real shields because the makers "have been making shields with such clear intent that they will strengthen and balance people, that this 'energy' goes into the shield with or without the actual crystals." She seemed surprised by this strange claim but also willing to accept it, and she recommended that we use shields made a different way for our next experiments. Indeed, she kindly had a new set of three real and three fake shields made especially. Using these we carried out two further experiments to find out whether the shields protect people from the weakening effects of holding a mobile phone (cell phone). The results suggest they do not.

I had started this study with the opinion that someone somewhere was maliciously and greedily making false claims to take money from vulnerable people. I ended up with quite a different view—that well-meaning people were selling a product they genuinely believed in to people who also believed in it and felt better, even though the specific claims are false. You might argue that as long as people feel better no harm is done, but the harm is that the effects of a powerful placebo can lead people to adopt a demonstrably false, and even antiscientific, view of the world. . . .

Skeptics Cling to Beliefs, Too

Skepticism is the focus of many skeptics' lives. Some have committed their careers to promoting skepticism and to debunking paranormal claims. Would they find it easy to change their minds if good evidence for the paranormal came along? I think not. The problem in making this comparison is that there is, as far as I can tell, no good evidence for the paranormal. Nevertheless, some skeptics display just the same reluctance to change, and tendency to biased interpretations, as the most ardent believers do. In skeptical books and magazines we can read again and again authors who prefer to accept even the feeblest and least well founded skeptical explanation of a claim, rather than consider the possibility that the claim might be true. Yet if we are going to study psychic claims at all, we must always consider the possibility that they are true. Unlikely as it is, ESP and PK [psychokinesis] might exist. There could be forces as yet undiscovered. We should accept the best explanation we can find—not the one that we like the most. The lesson we should learn . . . is not that believers find it hard to be open-minded but that we all do.

Not only is it emotionally taxing to consider our least favorite theories, but it is hard work too. It takes a lot of time and effort to make a reasonably fair and unbiased assessment of any paranormal claim. I knew I was no longer prepared to do it properly when one day a huge pile of papers arrived in the post. The Stargate [a government program researching psychic phenomena] affair had just broken. The evidence coming out of all the Stanford Research Institute remote-viewing work was published and various people were arguing about whether it did, or did not, provide evidence for psi [parapsychological phenomena]. Several people asked for my opinion and a friend sent me a huge packet containing all the information. I balked. I was not prepared to be an ignorant parapsychologist/skeptic and give opinions on experiments I had not studied. I knew that I would be prepared to give an opinion—whether publicly or privately—only if I had read all that material. And I knew that I did not want to read it. . . .

What then of parapsychology? The world still might be as I imagined it at the start and because the implications would be so profound I am glad that others are carrying on. The recent resurgence of funding for parapsychology means there are several new labs and many new researchers at work. If psi does exist then one day one of them will find a way to demonstrate it and a theory to explain it. If that happens I shall be back like a shot, but until then, happily, I have given up.

> *"Explicit instruction that explores para-
> normalism and teaches skepticism in
> that context can decrease students' be-
> liefs in paranormal phenomena and in-
> crease their tendency to think skepti-
> cally."*

Education Influences Belief in Paranormal Phenomena

Michael J. Dougherty

*Dr. Michael Dougherty is an associate professor of biology at
Hampden-Sydney College in Virginia. His teaching interests include the Human Genome Project and other topics in molecular
biology and biochemistry, as well as skepticism about paranormal topics. In the following viewpoint, Dr. Dougherty describes
an experiment conducted at Hampden-Sydney College to mea-
sure how skeptical education influenced the belief in paranormal
phenomena held by members of the freshman class.*

As you read, consider the following questions:

1. What external factors might have skewed the data of the
   experiment?
2. What is the Skeptical Index and how is it generated?

Michael J. Dougherty, "Educating Believers," *Skeptic*, vol. 10, 2004, pp. 31–35. Reproduced by permission.

3. What is the Forer Effect and how does it contribute to belief in paranormal phenomena?

An individual may claim to have seen a ghost and may accept that isolated paranormal event as valid, yet that event may not affect the individual in any obvious way beyond, say, reporting it to others on occasion. Other individuals see the world more generally through metaphysical lenses that include paranormal interpretations as part of the typical field of view. In either case, entrenched paranormal beliefs in one area may predispose individuals to interpret other events as paranormal rather than naturalistic or scientific—a supposition supported by the observation that paranormal beliefs cluster in individuals. From the standpoint of science literacy, it is the predisposition to paranormalism, rather than the relatively isolated incidents, that poses the most significant challenge for educators, for it may limit the ability of the paranormally inclined to participate effectively in a society where science and skepticism are dominant.

Fortunately, it appears that explicit instruction that explores paranormalism and teaches skepticism in that context can decrease students' beliefs in paranormal phenomena and increase their tendency to think skeptically. In this paper, I will describe the results of a study of student beliefs and how they changed as a result of a course on skepticism and the paranormal.

Design of the Study

As part of a pilot study, a one-semester course entitled *Alien Abductions, Crop Circles, and Psychics: Caveat Credulous* (Skep-185), was developed at Hampden-Sydney College [H-SC] as part of the freshmen seminar program. The course enrolled 11 freshmen males (H-SC is an all-male institution), a typical number for that type of course, and 10 participated in two surveys administered to track beliefs.

A belief survey was developed based on an adaptation of a 2001 Gallup poll, made up of 13 paranormal beliefs (psychic healing, ESP, haunted houses, the Devil, ghosts, telepathy, ET, clairvoyance, talking to the dead, astrology, witches, reincarnation, and channeling). To encourage participation of faculty and students in control classes, the survey was simple, brief, and anonymous. Students were instructed to choose one of the following responses to characterize their view toward each belief: Believe, Not Sure, or Don't Believe. Completion of the survey took approximately five minutes. The pre-course survey (pre-survey) was administered on the first day of class. The identical survey was also administered to three freshmen Rhetoric classes, with a total enrollment of 31 students. Those classes served as controls for evaluating the role that skepticism instruction might play in altering beliefs. In the last week of the semester, the identical survey was given to all sections (post-survey). During the semester, the control classes developed the skills necessary to compose a written argument while the skepticism class actively learned about the characteristics of paranormal thinking and skeptical habits of mind.

Preliminary Results

Several beliefs stand out for their relatively high and low beliefs tendencies among the students. Of the paranormal beliefs offered, haunted houses and ghosts were the ones students appeared most likely to believe, with spiritual healing, ESP, and telepathy rating high as well. Substantially more students in Skep-185 than the control classes indicated belief in visits by aliens, which may be a selection effect. (The abbreviated course title, as it appeared on the course-registration schedule, was *Alien Abduction.*) A substantially larger number of control students than Skep-185 students indicated that they were unsure about visits by aliens. Moreover, the percentage in each group who did not believe in alien visits was approximately the same. Belief in astrology rated lowest among the beliefs and lower than is typically found in the general population, a finding that is likely related to the fact that all of the participants were male. Gallup polls consistently indicate that women are somewhat more likely than men to believe in astrology, and to have visited psychics and fortune tellers. Students in both groups were particularly disinclined to believe in channeling, possession by the Devil and witches.

The mean and standard deviation for each group by belief tendency were quite similar, suggesting that the two populations were the same at the beginning of the study. To statistically compare the pre-survey populations, however, it was necessary to develop a metric summarizing responses across all paranormal beliefs—a "skepticism index"—for each individual student, and to compare the two groups based on those indices. To generate the skepticism index, each survey (representing an individual student) was scored by assigning the following values for each belief item: Believe=1, Not sure=3, and Don't believe=5. Thus, an average score of one corresponds to maximum credulity, and a score of five indicates maximum skepticism. (Note: A one-to-five scale was used to aid presentation of results. A one-to-three scale yielded similar statistical outcomes.) Total scores were averaged for each student, and then the pre-survey population were compared statistically. The mean skepticism index was nearly identical for each group (3.26 and 3.28 for the Skep-185 and control classes, respectively), and the range of scores was also very similar. Statistical analysis. . . supported the null hypothesis that the populations of the students in the paranormal/skepticism class and the control classes were indeed the same at the beginning of the semester.

At the end of the semester, data from the post-survey were compiled. The results showed that the overall skepticism did not change in the control classes. As predicted, the skepticism index for the Skep-185 class increased 45% over the pre-survey class average (3.26). This change was significant. . . .

A Pairwise Comparison

The preliminary study prompted the teaching of a second course (HONS 101) to compare belief changes by individual students rather than classes. The second seminar course used the same survey and methodology, although a second instructor (a psychologist) participated and some additional readings were added. Anonymous, coded surveys were used to correlate students' responses on the pre- and post-surveys. That course also was composed exclusively of freshmen (n-17), but those men were admitted as part of the honors program. Interestingly, their average skepticism index was lower than the original control population (2.99 vs. 3.28) although the difference was not significant.

[There were] changes in skepticism toward the particular beliefs surveyed from the beginning of the course to the end. Skepticism toward every paranormal belief increased, with increases ranging from 19 to 144%, although only six of those changes were significant . . . (spiritual healing, ESP, ghosts, alien visitation, clairvoyance, and astrology). One additional belief (possession by the Devil) was significant. . . . The biggest changes were observed for the existence of ghosts and visitations by aliens (skepticism up 112% and 144%, respectively). Taken together, the overall change in the skepticism index for all students in the class, by pairwise comparison, was from 2.99 to 3.93, an increase of 47%.

A student-by-student analysis revealed that of the 12 students with skepticism indices less than or equal to 3.0 (about 70% of the class)—values indicating much room for potential increases in skepticism—the average increase was 69%. Interestingly, three of those students improved less than 10% (in one case not at all). Those students may represent a background population of students who will remain resistant to change even with focused educational efforts such as those described here. The remaining five students (those with indices of greater than 3.0) were substantially skeptical at the begin-

From *50 Things You Can Do to Encourage Critical Thinking*

Having a skeptical mind is great. But if your idea of encouraging skeptical thinking is to argue with anybody you can find, you might not be using your critical reasoning abilities to their fullest potential. There are a lot of opportunities out there to help other people develop an understanding of science and an awareness of skepticism. Here are a few ways you can can have a positive impact on your community.

• With the co-operation of your local university science departments, create a science telephone line for the media to call with questions.

• Create a similar line for the general public.

• Prepare fact sheets on health fraud and quackery and give them to doctors' offices, hospitals and church groups to distribute.

• Encourage local mental health professionals to talk to groups on the importance of dealing with grief appropriately.

• Arrange showings of skeptic documentaries . . . at your local library or community center.

• Arrange field trips for grown ups to science museums.

Andrew Mayne,
"50 Things You Can Do to Encourage Critical Thinking,"
Skeptic, vol. 11, 2004, p. 26. Reproduced by permission.

ning of the course and thus had much less room for improvement. Nonetheless, even those students demonstrated an average increase in skepticism of 18%, from 3.92 to 4.44.

The Paranormalism/Skepticism Curriculum

The curriculum used in teaching about paranormalism and skepticism was based primarily on readings from several books, as well as films, videos, in-class exercises, and formal papers written by students. The first third of the course was primarily an exploration of different paranormal phenomena, with special focus on psychic predictions, alien visits and abductions, astrology, and numerology. The classes discussed first-hand experiences with these phenomena and reviewed Web and newspaper accounts.

The instructor also engaged in elaborate ruses to demonstrate his own purported paranormal abilities, under the guise of establishing credibility as an instructor of such a course. For example, he provided a demonstration of claimed telepathic abilities, using mathematical manipulations to "read" numbers held in students' minds, and used his telekinetic powers to reverse the spin direction of the propeller on the familiar "hooey" stick. As this author demonstrated, with practice such tricks can be performed convincingly by non-magicians, and, surprisingly, they confound and amaze even the brightest students. Additional demonstrations included astrological readings, numerology, and the generation of predictions hidden in texts having nothing to do with events predicted (a variation on the Bible codes theme). Those demonstrations established for all the students some common experiences with apparently paranormal phenomena. The intent was to use those experiences, along with information from readings and videos, to create some cognitive dissonance—the sense that your beliefs or intuition do not match what is actually true. Students' initial reactions to the demonstrations suggested that this goal was accomplished as some immediately were troubled by the incongruity posed by a (supposedly) talented psychic working as a biology professor rather than as a practicing paranormalist.

The middle third of the course began to explore the differences between skeptical thinking and paranormalism. It was at this time that students became aware of the psychological and behavioral tendencies that many paranormalists capitalize on, such as the Forer Effect—the tendency for people to interpret vague statements about personal characteristics as unique to themselves. This point was driven home when the students discovered that all of their supposedly personalized horoscopes (which the students themselves rated as accurate) were in fact identical. They also began to question in earnest the legitimacy of the instructor's earlier demonstrations (e.g., psychic reading, telekinesis). Case studies of alien sightings and abductions introduced students to the nature of evidences, the fallibility of memory (e.g., hypnotic suggestibility), and the many circumstances under which even healthy individuals may hallucinate (e.g., hypnagogic imagery, sleep deprivation). Students also studied and discussed common logical fallacies.

As it moved into its final weeks, the course formalized the tenets of naturalistic methodologies in science, Hume's maxim regarding the nature of evidence, and the difference between causation and correlation. Students then examined the role paranormalism played (and continues to play) in religion, history, and economics. Discussions about "creation science," although threatening to some students, focused on the locus of controversy; trying to force supernatural explanations into the naturalistic and theory-based paradigm of science. Ultimately, the course considered the relationship between skepticism, paranormalism, free speech, and the nature of thinking and belief in a liberal democracy.

To encourage participation in the seminar discussions, the students were evaluated in large part on the thoughtfulness and frequency of their contributions, with class participation accounting for half of a student's final grade. Short assignments, such as finding some numerological significance in the letters of their own names, and three formal papers composed the remainder of the grade.

Conclusions

It is clear that many (perhaps most) college freshmen embark on their post-secondary careers predisposed to believe in phenomena that scientists reject as almost certainly false or unproven. More than half of the control students in this study had skepticism indices of 3 or less, indicating a greater tendency toward acceptance of paranormal phenomena than toward skepticism. And, not a single student in the control or experimental groups (n = 58) rejected belief in all of the paranormal phenomena at the beginning of the studies. This reinforces recent work documenting the prevalence of pseudoscientific beliefs among college students generally. Moreover, after one semester of exposure to the standard college curriculum (i.e., the control group), students were not likely to develop greater skepticism toward paranormal beliefs.

In other words, engaging in generalized "critical thinking" with ideas in the natural sciences, humanities, and social sciences may be insufficient to counter pre-existing paranormal beliefs—a hypothesis supported by the prevalence of paranormal beliefs among college graduates. By contrast, explicit instruction that forces students to confront the fragility of the evidence underlying their paranormal beliefs can make students, over the course of one semester, substantially more skeptical. In fact, two-thirds of the students in the experimental groups had skepticism indices of greater than 4 at the end of the course. Future work will examine the stability of the skepticism gains generated by these courses, by assessing paranormal beliefs at later points in the students' academic careers.

Writers such as Carl Sagan and Chet Raymo have argued that credulity adds nothing to the mystery of life that science cannot more adequately compensate. Sagan has also argued (along with Michael Shemer and others) that certain types of credulity may be harmful. For example, the pressure to inject creationism into the public school science curriculum is resurgent: people have gone to jail based on false (implanted) memories: and untested (and potentially unsafe) alternative medical therapies are a multibillion dollar business. At a minimum, the high rate of paranormal and pseudoscientific beliefs among adults mocks the scientific and naturalistic foundations of our society, technology, and economy. Although paranormal beliefs may be deeply ingrained and long standing, this study suggests that a relatively modest but focused educational effort may be sufficient to substantially reduce the tendency to hold paranormal beliefs.

> *"The biological basis of all spiritual and mystical experiences is due to spontaneous firing of the temporoparietal region—highly focal microseizures without any obvious motor effects."*

Brain Structure Influences Belief in Paranormal Phenomena

Dean Hamer

Dr. Dean Hamer is a geneticist at the National Cancer Institute at the National Institutes of Health. He studies how genes influence human behavior and personality. An author and a patent-holder, Hamer's work has appeared in many popular and academic science journals; he has also appeared on television talk shows, news programs, and documentaries. Hamer's book, The GOD Gene, attempts to pinpoint the source of a person's religious faith within the structure of the brain. The following viewpoint is an excerpt that describes the similarities among mystical visions experienced by famous prophets and spiritual leaders, and compares the physical sensations to those triggered during an episode of temporal lobe epilepsy.

As you read, consider the following questions:

1. What specific symptoms of temporal lobe epilepsy (TLE) resemble descriptions of spiritual visions?

2. Why do people with TLE sometimes assume they are having a mystical experience instead of an epileptic seizure?

3. To what does the term "God spot" refer?

What did the apostle Paul, Muhammad the prophet, Joan of Arc, and Fyodor Mikhailovich Dostoyevsky have in common? All of them were intensely religious. All of them had mystical visions. And some scientists now think all of them may have owed at least part of their intense feelings of spirituality to temporal lobe epilepsy, a neurological disease that causes abnormal electrical firing in the limbic system.

Temporal lobe epilepsy is a common disorder, affecting about 2.5 million Americans. It is characterized by dreamy, hallucinatory seizures. Suddenly, for no apparent reason, the person becomes motionless and unresponsive. They seem frozen, but inside their heads the world is spinning. They may have visual alterations; lights seem to flash, and objects appear clearer or blurrier than normal, nearer or farther away. These visual effects are often accompanied by auditory illusions, including voices. Other sounds seem louder or softer than usual, or nearer or farther away. There also are emotional alterations; strong feelings of sorrow, joy, fear, or disgust well up without reason.

The most common sensation in temporal lobe seizures is that things just aren't quite the way they normally are. One psychiatrist had a patient who spent long periods staring at her coffee table because "it just doesn't look exactly like my coffee table." She didn't think the table actually changed, just her perception of it. Her consciousness was altered.

Historical Accounts

Physicians often miss temporal lobe epilepsy because it does not cause the dramatic convulsions of a grand mal seizure. The only way to make a sure diagnosis is for the person to spend weeks hooked up to an EEG machine [a device that measures brain activity] in a hospital ward. Obviously, we don't have electroencephalographs for Paul, Muhammad, Joan of Arc, or Dostoyevsky. There is, nevertheless, anecdotal evidence to suggest that each of them had temporal lobe epilepsy.

Paul had his most famous seizurelike experience when he was still Saul, a Jewish Pharisee traveling on the road to Damascus. According to the Bible, he saw a flash of light, fell down, and heard the voice of Christ. Afterward he was blind for several days. This episode has all the earmarks of an epileptic episode: Loss of balance, visual illusions, and auditory hallucinations are common in temporal lobe seizures. Blindness is rarer but has been reported in some cases.

If Paul had experienced just one episode on the road to Damascus, the diagnosis of temporal lobe epilepsy would be sketchy. But apparently it was part of a pattern. Paul later reported on an otherworldly trance that included "visions and revelations." His fellow apostle Luke reported that Paul had a "bodily weakness." In fact, many biblical scholars, including William James, believe that Paul suffered from epilepsy. His conversion experience was part of a persistent pattern, not a fluke.

Muhammad also had many seizurelike experiences; he saw flashing lights, heard the voices of the angel Gabriel and Allah, and suffered from fits of trembling and profuse sweating and bodily pain. He also had several out-of-body experiences, a common feature of temporal lobe epilepsy. Again, it was part of a lifelong pattern. Legend has it that Muhammad was born with excess fluid around the brain and had fits as a child.

Flashing lights and mysterious voices are two of the most common hallucinations in temporal lobe epilepsy. Joan of Arc experienced both:

> I heard this Voice to my right, towards the Church; rarely do I hear it without its being accompanied also by a light. This light comes from the same side as the Voice.

Joan had many such conversations with God, which guided her battle strategies.

Although Dostoyevsky is best known as a novelist, he was also an intensely spiritual person who believed that "man seeks not so much God as the miraculous." His interest in mystical experiences may have resulted from his epilepsy, which is documented in statements by his physicians, several biographies, and his own voluminous writing. Many of his fictional characters were tormented by their seizures, but Dostoyevsky enjoyed his—or at least the beginnings of them:

> You strong people have no idea of the bliss which epileptics experience in the moments preceding their attacks. For several moments, I have a feeling of happiness which I never experienced in my normal state and which one cannot imagine. It is a complete harmony in myself and in the wide world . . .

Non-Medical Consequences

The effects of temporal lobe epilepsy are not limited to the brief storms of electrical activity that occur during seizures. There are more abiding consequences. As noted by necrologist and psychiatrist Norman Geschwind, temporal lobe epileptics display many characteristic personality features even in the intervening periods between seizures. They often express an intense interest in philosophical issues and write about them extensively, a trait called hypergraphia. Sometimes they change their sexual preferences or lose their sex drive altogether. There is a tendency to imbue even ordinary scenes and events with emotional significance.

Symptoms of Temporal Lobe Epilepsy [TLE]

Somatosensory and Special Sensory Phenomena

- Auditory hallucinations consist of a buzzing sound, a voice or voices, or muffling of ambient sounds. This type of aura is more common with neocortical TLE than with other types of TLE.

- Patients may report distortions of shape, size, and distance of objects.

- Things may appear shrunken (micropsia) or larger (macropsia) than usual.

- Tilting of structures has been reported. Vertigo has been described with seizures in the posterior superior temporal gyrus.

Psychic Phenomena

- Patients may have a feeling of déjá vu or jamais vu, a sense of familiarity or unfamiliarity, respectively.

- Patients may experience depersonalization (i.e., feeling of detachment from oneself) or derealization (i.e., surroundings appear unreal).

- Fear or anxiety usually is associated with seizures arising from the amygdala. Sometimes, the fear is strong, described as an "impending sense of doom."

- Patients may describe a sense of dissociation or autoscopy in which they report seeing their own body from outside.

David Ko and Soma Sahai-Srivastava,
"Temporal Lobe Epilepsy," 2006. www.emedicine.com.

Most of all, they are hyperreligious. They attend religious services twice a day, build shrines in their homes, and have long conversations with God. They may give up their jobs and ignore their families to pursue their religious interests. They become zealots.

Now, clearly not every religious person has temporal lobe epilepsy—far from it—and not every temporal lobe epileptic becomes obsessed with religion. But the connection between the two is strong enough to make scientists wonder how it arises in the human brain.

The God Spot

Michael Persinger, a professor of psychology at Laurentian University in Canada who specializes in paranormal phenomena, thinks he knows the answer. Persinger had always been a nonbeliever. Then, in the course of using transcranial magnetic stimulation to study the function of various brain regions, he stimulated his own temporal and parietal lobes. For the first time in his life he experienced God. He had hit "The God Spot."

Based on this experiment and other lines of evidence, Persinger believes that the biological basis of all spiritual and mystical experiences is due to spontaneous firing of the temporoparietal region—highly focal microseizures without any obvious motor effects. He calls such episodes transients and theorizes that they occur in everybody to some extent. Exactly how often and how strongly is determined by a mix of genes, environment, and experience. The main effect of such transients is to increase communication between the right and left temporoparietal areas, leading to a brief confusion between the sense of self and the sense of others. The outcome, he says, is a "sense of a presence" that people interpret as a God, spirit, or other mystical being.

To test his theory, Persinger outfitted normal volunteers with a special helmet equipped with four sets of solenoids. He seated them in a quiet room, then stimulated their temporo-parietal areas with a magnetic field using either a biologically relevant waveform that mimicked the brain's own magnetic activity or, as a control, an irrelevant waveform that would not be expected to have any biological effect. The subjects were asked to press a button if they felt "a presence."

The results were just what Persinger predicted. The volunteers were significantly more likely to press the button when they received a biologically meaningful magnetic field than when they received no radiation or an irrelevant waveform. Some of the subjects even had mystical experiences. One female student reported a "feeling of rising" in which she was floating away into space, retained only by a thin thread.

Although Persinger's stimulation experiments are fascinating, they do have several flaws. One is suggestibility. Perhaps the subjects felt "a presence" only because they were told they might. This is especially troublesome since the volunteers were first-year psychology students who received a grade bonus for participating. ("Yeah, I felt the presence of God. Now do I get an A?")

The second problem is specificity. Does the experiment show that there is actually a "spot" or circuit in the brain that is devoted to spirituality, or does it simply reflect the side effects of stimulating regions normally involved in emotionality and self-recognition? It is hard to tell.

Another Approach

Neuroscientist V.S. Ramachandran took a different tack to find the "God spot." He hooked up electrodes to the hands of two temporal lobe epileptics with religious obsessions, showed them images and words on a computer screen, and recorded their skin response. When the subjects were shown familiar objects, like a picture of their parents or the word "shoe," there was no reaction. The same was true for portraits of strangers, erotic pinup shots, and four-letter words. Even the sight of a man being eaten alive by an alligator failed to get a response.

But when the temporal lobe epileptics were exposed to religious words and images, their skin responses went through the roof. Just seeing "God" on a computer screen was enough to set them off. All it took were a few well-chosen words and pictures to turn on the God spot in these individuals. By contrast, nonepileptic individuals showed just an average response to the religious symbols, reserving their strong responses for the sexual and violent scenes.

Ramachandran concluded that epilepsy caused permanent changes in the temporal lobe circuitry. Some circuits were enhanced, others diminished, leading to "new peaks and valleys in the patients' emotional landscape." The importance of his experiment is that it shows that the temporal lobe response is specific for religion. The electrical firestorms did not simply cause a general enhancement of emotion (a phenomenon called "kindling"); if that were the case, the epileptics would have responded more *strongly* to sexual and violent scenes, rather than more weakly. There was something about the way that God—or even the idea of God—made them feel that changed in their brain.

| "Scientists studying human development have already described at least 12 major levels of consciousness."

People Are Interconnected by a Collective Consciousness

Robert Kenny

Robert Kenny is a faculty member of the California Institute of Integral Studies. He specializes in executive coaching, leadership development, and helping people build creativity and wisdom teams in their personal and professional lives. Kenny describes, "collective consciousness is a mode of awareness that emerges at the first transpersonal stage of consciousness, when our identities expand beyond our egos. A crucial capacity that accompanies this awareness is the ability to intuitively sense and work with the interactions between our and others' energy fields, physically, emotionally, mentally and spiritually. . . . More of us are now becoming aware of our capacity not only to intuit each other's thoughts and emotions, but also to consciously think and create together without communicating through our five senses." In the following viewpoint, he describes the scientific research that supports the existence of a collective consciousness.

Robert Kenny, M.B.A., "What Can Science Tell Us about Collective Consciousness?" Excerpt retrieved and edited February 13, 2008, from http://www.collectivewisdom initiative.org/papers/kenny_science.htm. Copyright © 2004, Robert Kenny and Leaderful Teams Consulting. Reproduced by permission of the author.

This chapter is excerpted from a sixty-four-page monograph, which can be found at the URL listed in the table of contents. The chapter does not include the specific citations or references contained in the online document, which may be of interest to students who wish to write an academic and scientific paper, or who wish to explore the phenomenon of collective consciousness and collective wisdom more extensively.

As you read, consider the following questions:

1. What termite behavior suggests that these insects may communicate collectively?
2. What are some ways that people have been able to remotely influence the behavior of cells and organisms?
3. What changes were effected in Israel in 1983 when a group of people in the surrounding area meditated together?

A number of researchers have argued that individuals and groups can influence each other outside of modalities of communication that use the five senses, through some form of field effect. This is not a wild or unfounded suggestion: magnetic, electrical and gravitational fields are all invisible, yet capable of bringing about effects at a distance. In biology, the concept of morphogenetic fields, underlying the form of a growing organism, is widely accepted, yet scientists don't yet know what these fields are or how they work. Successful sports-team members refer to a sixth sense, empathy, and an ability to anticipate the moves of the other; or to a "click of communality," an almost audible shift whereby sports participants react as a . . . unit, rather than as an aggregate of individuals. . . . If the members of a group or team have established a sense of trust, a warm emotional connection, and an inspiring, shared purpose, they can perform tasks fluidly, efficiently and in a highly coordinated state, with minimal verbal communication or visual contact. . . .

Insect and Animal Coordination and Nonsensory Communication

[Biologist Rupert] Sheldrake considers animal societies to be social morphic units, which "provides a way of understanding the coordination of the behavior of individual organisms within the social unit: the colony, school, flock, herd, pack, group, or pair." For example, he and other researchers have concluded that the behavior of the members of termite colonies are coordinated by social fields, which contain the blueprints for the construction of the colony, and pass through physical barriers. Experiments have indicated that neither sense-mediated communication nor an electrical field can likely explain how termites, after the nest they are building is cut in half and separated by a steel plate, can still go on to create structures and tunnels that are perfectly aligned. Consequently, Sheldrake has concluded that in termite colonies

> "the individual insects are coordinated by social fields, which contain the blueprints for the construction of the colony.... To make models without taking such fields into account is rather like trying to explain the behavior of iron filings around a magnet [while] ignoring the field, as if the pattern somehow 'emerged' from programs within the individual iron particles." ...

In the case of termite nests, the workers first make columns, then bend them toward each other at some point and join them at a midpoint between the two columns. Termites are blind, so they cannot make this happen through visual alignment. Researchers have concluded that the coordination does not happen through movement back and forth between the columns, to get an alignment through measurement, nor does it seem that sound plays a part. And, as Sheldrake points out,

> "Smell can hardly account for the overall plan of the nest or the relationship of the individual insects to it. They seem to

'know' what kind of structure is required; they seem to be responding to a kind of invisible plan. As [biologist Edwin] Wilson phrased the question, 'Who has the blueprint of the nest?' I suggest that this plan is embodied in the organizing field of the colony. This field is not inside the individual insects; rather, they are inside the collective field. Just as a magnetic field can pass through material structures, so [must] the colony field. This ability. . .would enable the field to organize separated groups of termites even in the absence of normal sensory communication between them." . . .

[Researcher Eugene] Marais separated termite mounds into two halves and inserted a steel plate, which was a few feet wider and higher than the termitary, into the breach of each mound, thereby preventing all sensory and electrical means of communication. Despite this, the termites still built a similar arch on either side of the plate, which were aligned. Sheldrake commented:

"The repair activity seemed to be coordinated by some overall organizing structure, which Marais attributed to the group soul, and I prefer to think of as a morphic field. . . . Unlike the field investigated by [Gunther] Becker, it was not blocked by a metal plate, and was therefore unlikely to be electrical in nature." . . .

Sheldrake and others have demonstrated that psi capacities are widely distributed in the animal kingdom. [Psi (or teleprehension, as Ken Wilber calls it) is extra-sensory perception or influence, perhaps made possible by the apparent ability of consciousness to operate beyond the constraints of space and time. Examples include telepathy and remote viewing.] In a series of experiments, he showed how certain pets sensed when their owners decided to return home from work or an excursion, even when they varied the time from day to day.

Sheldrake argues that humans have partly lost or neglected the psi capacities that animals demonstrate, and that . . . they are not paranormal or supernatural abilities. . . .

Heart to Brain Communication

A relatively new arena of research is called energy cardiology or cardioelectromagnetic communication. The heart's electrical field is measured with an electrocardiogram (ECG). The magnetic component of the heart's field is not impeded by tissues and can be measured several feet away from the body. Under certain conditions, the heart's electromagnetic waves synchronize with the brain waves (measured by the electroencephalogram or EEG) of oneself or other human and non-human animals.

For example, heart-focused attention is correlated with greater synchronization of heart and brain. Sustained positive emotions, such as appreciation, love, or compassion, are associated with highly ordered or coherent patterns in the heart rhythms and a shift in autonomic balance toward increased parasympathetic activity. This "physiological coherence" is the state of "more ordered and harmonious interactions among the body's systems." Cross coherence occurs when "two or more of the body's oscillatory systems, such as respiration and heart rhythms, become entrained and oscillate at the same frequency." When individuals were taught how to use a positive-emotion refocusing technique to generate appreciation, cross-coherence significantly increased. It was expressed as a higher ratio of alpha rhythms in the brain (measured by the EEG) that was synchronized with the heartbeat (measured by the ECG). Increased physiological coherence is correlated with a number of health and mental health benefits. In the converse, experimental evidence suggests that certain prolonged negative psychological states can facilitate the progression of cancer and increase risk for physical illness and early death.

As I report elsewhere in this paper, a number of studies have found that subtle energies used by healers are correlated with increased wound healing rates, lowered pain, increased hemoglobin levels, conformational changes of DNA and water structure, and changes in psychological states. . . .

Heart to Heart Communication

Although the number of subjects is still too small to reliably generalize, researchers at HeartMath have found that the heart rates of people who have a close living or working relationship, and who generate feelings of appreciation for each other while sitting four feet apart (and being blind to the data), can become entrained. This entrainment apparently also occurs during sleep, between couples that have been in long-term, stable and loving relationships. Their heart rhythms can converge and can simultaneously change in the same direction. Another study found that the heart rates of married couples, who were skilled at empathizing, became synchronized and tracked each other during empathetic interactions. Despite some methodological problems, several studies have suggested that entrainment may also occur during empathetic interactions between therapists and clients.

These results regarding cardioelectromagnetic communication indicate the importance of relationship-centered approaches to not only clinical and professional care, but also to team and organizational development. Based upon training thousands of people to maintain coherence during conversation, HeartMath researchers have concluded

> "It is a common experience that they become more attuned to other people and are able to detect and understand the deeper meaning behind spoken words . . . , even when the other person may not be clear. . . . Intuitive listening helps people to feel fully heard and promotes greater rapport and empathy between people."

The proposed interpersonal communication mechanisms may in part explain the *positive* effects of service and care that emphasize the relational aspects of human interaction in professional settings. . . .

Brain to Brain Communication

Despite the typical methodological issues that need to be worked out in any new area of research, a number of experiments have indicated that "tele-prehension" of thoughts, images, emotions, intuitions and physical sensations between persons is facilitated when people are bound by close emotional ties and empathy (e.g., "bonded couples" or monozygotic twins), are in an altered state of consciousness, or meditate together, although this effect occurs in other situations, too. The respective EEG brain wave patterns of pairs become highly synchronized or coherent. EEG alpha rhythms . . . (measured by a functional MRI machine) created in one person can produce the same effects in another, even when members of a pair are separated in sound-attenuated or electromagnetically shielded rooms. In addition, in several experiments, individual interhemispheric synchronization occurred (a phenomena that happens during meditation) when paired participants tried to sense each other's presence while in separate rooms. Moreover, the individual with the greatest synchronization tended to influence the other member of the pair. . . .

Nonlocal, Intentional Influence

A large number of studies has examined the ability of people to influence other living beings in remote settings. In a series of experiments, for example, influencers changed the direction of knife fish, got gerbils to run faster on activity wheels, and slowed the rate of hemolysis (bursting of cell walls) in red blood cells. In 16 remote staring trials, starees showed significantly greater electrodermal activity (EDA) while being stared at (59%, versus 50% chance), indicating that they had unconsciously felt the attention of the starers. These results have been replicated a number of times. A meta-analysis reported a significant effect size in experiments where the receiver's skin conductance was targeted. Remote intention has been shown to have a significant calming effect on a group of highly nervous people, and to help participants focus their attention, especially those whose attention tended to wander. In some cases during these studies, telepathy occurred. A number of these findings have been replicated, including intention's effect upon healing.

A meta-analysis has shown that intention can affect a wide range of living organisms, including their healing. Moreover, studies have demonstrated that a group can significantly influence the eye or gross motor movements, breathing and brain rhythms of a different group. Although the effects were small in scale, ordinary people, who were trying remote influence for the first time, consistently produced them. The EDA studies succeeded 47% of the time and the studies in general had the intended effect 37% of the time, in contrast to an expected 5% chance success rate. Distance seemed irrelevant, with effects extending even into outer space, during a space mission. The greatest influence occurred when the subjects greatly needed the intended effect, which indicates that healing interactions may be particularly effective. Finally, as with other forms of tele-prehension, strength of effect correlated with how much the influencer related to the subject, increasing as the subjects changed from animals, to human cells, to other people. This finding is consistent with [the] assertion that humans share a greater number of fields (and subtler fields) with each other, than they share with animals, for example, thereby increasing the means and strength of influence. . . .

Social and Cultural Healing

Groups of Transcendental Meditation (TM) practitioners have had significant impact upon the well being and physical and mental health of surrounding geographic communities. . . . [Fifty] very rigorous, socially focused, scientific studies, which have controlled for alternative explanations, have been con-

Particle Physics Describe Schools of Fish

Basing their work on a particle-interaction model from physics, [Oxford scientist Iain Couz and his team] represented each fish as a single particle. They assumed three rules about how the particles interact: Each fish tries to avoid colliding with other fish, stays with the group, and aligns its swimming direction with that of nearby fish within some defined zone around itself. . . .

The researchers also assumed that fish can modify their sensitivity to their neighbors, that is, the size of their alignment zones. The team found that as the individuals' alignment zones grow, the school's architecture undergoes two sharp transitions.

When the alignment zone around each fish is negligible in size, so that the fish barely pay attention to their neighbors' directions, each fish swims in a random direction within the group. At a certain critical size of the alignment zone, the fish suddenly start following each other to produce a doughnut-shaped swarm. As the alignment zone continues to grow, the fish start swimming in parallel, as in a migration. . . .

The model shows that simple rules for how fish interact with their neighbors can give rise to complex, schoolwide patterns. Couzin reports, "There's nothing in the individual rules that says, 'Go in a circle,' but it happens spontaneously."

Erica Klarreich,
Science News Online, November 25, 2006.
www.sciencenews.org.

ducted over more than 30 years. Many of the experiments have been published in well respected, peer-reviewed scientific journals. The results have been impressive, in terms of improved quality of life and health and decreased crime rate, accidents, war, etc. I cite some of these studies below. . . .

A 1993 study found that, when 4,000 people meditated together, violent crime in Washington, D.C., declined 23% over the course of the experiment, in contrast to its rising in the months before and after. The results were shown not to be due to other variables, such as weather, the police, or anti-crime campaigns. The predicted effect had been posited with an independent review board, which had participated in the study design and monitored its conduct. A similar effect was shown in a study of 24 U.S. cities, in which 1% of the urban population regularly practiced TM. A follow-up study demonstrated that the 24 cities saw drops of 22% in crime and 89% in the crime trend, compared to increases of 2% and 53%, respectively, in the control cities.

During a two-month period in 1983 in Israel, on days when a TM-Sidhi group [advanced practitioners of Transcendental Meditation] equaling the square root of 1% of the surrounding population meditated, independently published data showed that war-related deaths in Lebanon dropped 76%, and conflict, traffic fatalities, fires and crime decreased. In Israel, the national mood increased, as measured by a blinded content analysis of the emotional tone of the lead, front-page picture story in the *Jerusalem Post*, and the stock market increased. Other potential causal variables were controlled for. Predictions regarding war-reduction in Lebanon and increased quality of life in Israel had been posited with two independent project review board of scientists before the experiments began. The study was subsequently repeated seven times, with statistically significant effects. Research in five conflict-ridden locations around the globe, in the U.S., and worldwide (via TM-Sidhi assemblies of 7,000 practitioners, equal to the square root of 1% of the world's population in the mid-1980s) produced similar effects. . . .

Developing Collective Consciousness

According to the Vedanta and Vajrayana wisdom traditions, only when individuals have consciously developed a particular, sustainable level of consciousness can they permanently realize, access and master the correlated states of consciousness and behaviors, thereby "converting 'temporary states' to 'permanent traits.'" ... Individuals who develop sustainable, transpersonal levels of consciousness (wherein their identity extends beyond themselves, to include other sentient beings and the environment)—whether through a conversion experience or ongoing reflective or spiritual practice—seem to be able to express collective consciousness relatively consistently. At some point, they experience what I call a "communion of the heart." They begin to evidence ongoing care for the common good and to exhibit collaborative intention and skills regularly, no matter what situation they are in, and no matter what group, organization, or community they are involved with.

We now stand at a critical juncture, where we can begin to correlate the findings of the wisdom and scientific traditions. By stripping most metaphysical constructs from the wisdom-tradition model of consciousness in his recent work, the philosopher, Ken Wilber, has opened more of the model's stages to scientific investigation. Scientists studying human development have already described at least 12 major levels of consciousness, which can be studied in at least 24 developmental lines. ... To realize the individual and social benefits of developing collective consciousness and wisdom, which have been suggested by the research described in this paper and by applied disciplines such as organizational and community development, we need to learn how to develop sustainable collaborative capacities and skills. ...

We will only be able to develop and utilize our collective wisdom through consistent practice, self-honesty and courage.

Research regarding the means for developing collective consciousness is therefore crucial.

> "Human beings are very easily im-
> pressed. What seems utterly unlikely to
> a human being often turns out to be
> extremely probable in the cosmic
> scheme of things."

People Appear to Be Interconnected Because of Coincidence

Martin Plimmer and Brian King

Martin Plimmer is a journalist, broadcaster, and novelist. Brian King creates documentaries and produces programs for BBC Radio. Their collaboration, the book Beyond Coincidence, *attempts to explain why people are so interested in coincidences and how science and mathematics explain them. The following viewpoint explores how coincidence has been perceived and interpreted throughout history, and argues that coincidences seem to happen more frequently in modern times because—thanks to technological innovations—humans interact with so many different people.*

As you read, consider the following questions:

1. What elements of the modern world make it more prone to episodes of coincidence?

2. Why are "acausal" explanations of coincidence often rejected by the people who experience it?

3. What do psychologists mean by the phrase "illusion of control"?

The oldest observed and most enchanting coincidence of nature has led wise men and children a merry dance down the ages to many and various inventive explanations. It is the fact that the Sun and the Moon appear equal in size in our sky. We know now it's all a matter of perspective, but that's only because clever people have told us so.

The first clever people had very little reliable knowledge to build upon. The 6th-century-BC Greek philosopher Heraclitus estimated the Sun to be a foot in diameter. This would have made its distance from Earth around forty-four yards. It's easy to say now, with the help of five minutes' research on the Internet, that Heraclitus was wrong. We can even give him the figures: the Sun is 830,247 miles across, compared with 2085 miles for the Moon. The Sun's diameter is four hundred times larger than the Moon's. The Sun is also four hundred times farther away from us than the Moon. It is this relative distance that makes the two bodies equal in size in our perception.

Given the apparent randomness of the cosmos and the vast distances involved, it is a truly remarkable coincidence that from our unique perspective the Sun and the Moon should appear the same. But coincidence is all it is, however potent the Sun and Moon's symbolism in our lives and folklore as a complementary pair of equal opposites.

What was magical in the past, however, doesn't necessarily hold the same mystery for us now. On the other hand we are not immune to magical interpretations of newly perceived coincidences. In fact the evidence suggests that our tendency to opt for paranormal explanations is increasing. One reason is that we experience a lot more coincidences than people did in the past, and the frequency multiplies every year.

Modern Society Facilitates Coincidence

Our ancestors lived in smaller communities than ours, traveled less frequently, less far, and were exposed to a narrower range of experiences. Opportunities for unlikely correlations in their lives were more limited. They made the most of those that came their way, often investing them with profound significance.

Ostensibly the modern world is less superstitious, yet it is also a place in which seeming magic is more likely to happen. It's a busy and bewildering place, growing ever busier and more bewildering. Within the last hundred years human society has accommodated several dynamic technological revolutions, each of which has transformed the pace and scope of individual experience. We now have mass mobility, mass communication, and mass access to computing power; and we have that inexhaustible information regurgitator, the Internet.

The solemn maxim "know thyself," written above the temple of the Ancient Greek oracle at Delphi, may be—as it ever was—more honored in the breach than in the observance, but now at least we seem to know everything else. There are billions of items of computer-sorted information at everybody's fingertips, broadening our view but not necessarily our understanding.

Profligacy of information makes the possibility of coincidence more likely. The statistician's law of large numbers states that if the sample is very large even extremely unlikely things become likely. Well, the sample base we expose ourselves to every time we travel abroad or log on to the Internet is vast. "It's a small world!" we exclaim, as the correlations come together. One thing is certain: the wider the World Wide Web, the smaller the world. Today we are wired for coincidence.

More Feasible than Fantastic

But while our experience of coincidence has increased, our knowledge of probability hasn't kept pace. Most of us have a better grasp of elementary mathematics than did the average American colonist, but the sheer volume and complexity of our experience of coincidence makes it harder than ever to sort out the fantastic from the mathematically feasible.

That's why the most consistent factor of reported coincidences is the insistence by their observers that they aren't coincidences at all. They are brought about by angels, or magic, or sock goblins, or space aliens playing around with the postal services—anything but simple chance.

The problem is, chance isn't simple. You need to know a fair bit of mathematics to be able to work out probabilities. Scientists and bookies do it inside their cool heads but most of the rest of us are dismayed by the arithmetical effort and rely instead on intuition, which is demonstrably bad at estimating probability. Human beings are very easily impressed. What seems utterly unlikely to a human being often turns out to be extremely probable in the cosmic scheme of things. Think Sun and Moon.

The Coincidence of Prophecy

Or think Bible codes. According to some ancient accounts, the Book of Genesis in the Hebrew Bible, which is said to have been dictated by God himself, contains codes that if deciphered will reveal many other messages for mankind. It has long been a respectable pursuit for scholars belonging to remote and dusty religious orders to attempt to detect hidden patterns therein, discounting the spaces and punctuation in the text and treating the letters as a regular matrix. Inevitably, given the number of letters the Bible contains, and the fact that written Hebrew contains no vowels, many coincidental word patterns have manifested themselves in these searches, to which significant meaning has been attributed.

Computer science, far from making this arcane procedure seem even more eccentric, kicked the whole code detection business into a different league by increasing the speed and the variety of ways in which the letter matrix could be analyzed. Words could be identified running forward, backward, vertically, and diagonally in the text. Using a procedure called equivalent letter spacing it could also find words consisting of letters that were not adjacent, but were spread out in the text, each letter separated by the same number of non-relevant letters. Computer searches carried out by the prominent Israeli mathematician Professor Eliyahu Rips discovered incredible examples of conceptually related words adjacent to each other in the text, such as the names and birthplaces of famous rabbis. The discovery of the name of the murdered Israeli president Yitzhak Rabin next to a reference to death and a vertical "Kennedy" running through the phrase "assassin that will assassinate" seemed to suggest a prophetic quality.

Skeptics were slow to counter the claims of the researchers and Michael Drosnin's book about the phenomenon, *The Bible Code*, sold millions. Even today it seems few things excite us more than the prospect of proof of the paranormal. It took time for other teams of statisticians to find conceptual flaws in Professor Rips's painstakingly rigorous experiments. Meanwhile Brendan McKay, professor of computer science at the Australian National University, used Rips's system to find prophetic correlations of death and murdered presidents in *Moby-Dick*. In the end the Bible codes merely demonstrated that given enough letters, coincidental word patterns will emerge, and that many of them, given a little interpretation and a great deal of excitement, will appear to have meaning.

The Significance of One Person

In 1967, sociologist Stanley Milgram predicted that there were only six degrees of separation between any two people on the planet. The idea entered dinner party folklore, but few people realized that Milgram's attempts to prove it were unsuccessful. Recently, however, another sociologist, Duncan J. Watts, successfully proved a similar proposition. Watts assigned a thousand people a target person, possibly living in a different country and certainly from a different walk of life, and instructed them to attempt to pass an e-mail message to that person by forwarding it only to someone they knew, with a request to forward it on in the same way. On average it took between five and seven e-mails to hit the target.

Watts's experiment is an effective demonstration of the smallness of the world, but when incredible-seeming correlations happen to us outside of a scientific experiment they feel eerie and magical. There are many reasons why we might *want* them to be magical. The best is summed up by Richard Dawkins, a scientist famous for debunking the paranormal, who says, rather generously, given his standpoint, that we have a "natural and laudable appetite for wonder."

That appetite for wonder rekindled Joyce Simpson's faith in God. Joyce, of DeKalb County, Georgia, saw a sign in May 1991 that changed her life. To everyone else it was a Pizza Hut advertisement, but Joyce, who at the time was disillusioned enough with religion to be considering quitting her church choir, saw only salvation. Shining forth from a forkful of spaghetti was the face of Jesus.

A skeptic will say that if you look closely enough and with enough emotional motive you can see the face of God in any picture—spaghetti, chicken nuggets, deviled eggs—but there'd be no point telling Joyce Simpson that, nor the rapturous Georgians who lined up in their cars to see the billboard miracle for themselves once the news got out.

Assassinations Foretold in *Moby Dick!*

The following challenge was made by Michael Drosnin [author of the book, *The Bible Code*]:

When my critics find a message about the assassination of a prime minister encrypted in Moby Dick, I'll believe them. (Newsweek, June 9, 1997)

President Rene Moawad

```
L  O  W  M  A  L  E  I  N  T  H  A  T (M) A  T
(B)(U)(R)(S)(T)(O)(P)(E)(N)(T)(H)(E)(D)(O)(O)(R)
E  N  T  A  S  S  O  M  E  F  R  U  G (A) L  H
R  E  I  T  N  O  T  F  O  R  T  H  E (W) H  I
Y  E  W  H  A  T  M  E  N  O  L  D  R (A) D  S
C  R  I  M  I  N  A  T  I  O  N  A  N (D) T  H

(E)(N)(E)(R) A  L  L  Y  H  A  I  L  E (D) W  I  T
I  T  I  T  M  I  G  H  T  B  E  T  H (A) T  A  L
S  N  E  C  E  S  S  A  R  Y  O  N  T (W) O  A [C]
S  T  H  E  G  R  E  A  T  L  E  V  I [A] T  H  A
H  E  P  E  Q  U  O  D  S  T [R] Y  W (O) R  K  S
(A)(N)(E)(X)(P)(L)(O)(D)(I)(N)(G)(B)(O)(M)(B) U  P
```

Lebanese President Rene Moawad was killed Nov 22 1989 when a bomb exploded beside his car.

TAKEN FROM: Brendan McKay, "Assassinations Foretold in *Moby Dick!*" 1997. http://cs.anu.edu.au.

More or Less than Destiny?

Wonder engages the emotions. Wonder changes lives. Wonder makes you sit down and write that long postponed letter to Herbert Krantzer. "Dear Herbert. You won't believe this. I was washing my old VW Beetle, prior to finally selling the damn thing, and I found a note from you, dated June 1986, inside one of the hubcaps, wishing me a 'long and happy journey!' You must have slipped it in there on my wedding day all those years ago. . . ." It makes you feel especially blessed when Herbert writes back to say how good it was to receive your letter, particularly at that moment, for he is in the very process of finding an old VW Beetle for his son.

What made you take the hubcap off, for the first time in seventeen years, at that particular moment? To clean it, the skeptic will say. The letter finding event was acausal; in other words, you didn't find it *because* it might be propitious to contact an old friend at that particular point in time.

To most human beings this is a pretty bland interpretation. It's the word "acausal" that rankles. It renders what seemed full of wonder flat and dull. The letter writer may consider himself to be a rational thinker, but his mind is more interested in indulging the possibility that a guardian angel is smiling on him, or that his relationship with Herbert is so significant that some kind of telepathy is in play. He would rather take the agnostic "who knows?" position than consign it to mere chance.

Acausality doesn't do justice to the experience, especially when the experience is very personal. If a man dreams one night that his friend Moriarty is dying and then wakes up to be told that Moriarty has actually died, the notion that he may be psychic is extremely hard to resist. As is the notion that God sent him a warning to soften the blow, or that there are parallel universes in different time dimensions to which he might suddenly, because of the strength of his emotional compact with his friend, have gained access, or that the emotional right-hand side of the brain, containing a primitive intuitive consciousness suppressed by centuries of evolution, has woken up during his sleep, or that an event has come about because of the motivating power of his own thought process (on second thought, scrub that one). . . . There is no shortage of such explanations and every one of them is more interesting than arbitrary, impersonal, *acausal* chance. What makes them utterly irresistible is the way they engage the dreamer emotionally with the fact of the death: they impart a sense of having been present, or somehow consulted, at the end.

Chance vs. Glory

Statistician Christopher Scott has worked out the odds in the UK of dreaming of a friend's death the night it happens. Basing his calculation on fifty-five million people living an average of seventy years and experiencing one friend's death dream per lifetime, and then factoring in a national death rate of two thousand every twenty-four hours, Scott reckons there'll be an accurate death dream in Britain about every two weeks. It's human nature to recall only interesting stories, so accurate dreams are widely reported and frequently retold, while millions of dreams about dying friends who turn out the next day to be on the mend are routinely discarded from memory....

All explanations except chance grant the observer a starring role. Nowadays most of us tend to accept the skeptic's rationale, at least outwardly, but privately we like to at least flirt with the center-stage glory coincidence gives us. It's a natural enough desire that goes hand in glove with the need for an explanation for the universe that makes us feel less like a speck of random space dust and more like a cosmic player. Even the most skeptical probability mathematician, on finding a bottle washed up on a beach in Madagascar containing a note addressed to him, might be tempted to entertain that awesome possibility....

Two and a half thousand years ago, when Sophocles wrote *Oedipus Rex*, nobody was backward about predicting the future. They could research their destiny as readily as we can research our history and everyone had a direct line to the gods. Clotho, Lachesis, and Atropos sound like members of the

Marx Brothers, but to the average man they were very real, and not a bit funny. They were the three Fates, the indifferent celestial beings that meted out the thread of life apportioned to each mortal, decided on a few choice life qualities (tragedy, illness, etc.), and efficiently snipped it off at the due date. This thread was a man's *moira* (allotment). He couldn't erase the best-before date, nor could he escape his *moira's* negative elements, though he could, if he was foolish, make things much worse for himself.

Comets and other natural phenomena were obvious augurs; not cosmic coincidences these, but harbingers of specific events on Earth, usually disasters. The fall of Jerusalem, the death of Julius Caesar, and the defeat of the English by William the Conqueror were all said to have been augured by comets. King Harold's defeat was mapped out by Halley's comet. It came around again in 1986, presaging what evil this time? The explosion of the space shuttle *Challenger?* The assassination of Swedish prime minister Olof Palme? The invasion of the United States by [the movie sensation] *Crocodile Dundee?*

It's unusual to make such association today, yet a minority of people still do. It's not hard to find clairvoyant sites on the Internet asserting cast-iron connections between historical events and comet appearances that preceded them. The astronomer Carl Sagan, who waged a war against "baloney and pseudoscience," said that since human history is intrinsically unhappy, "any comet at any time, viewed from anywhere on Earth is assured of some tragedy for which it can be held accountable." . . .

Masters of the Universe

Psychologists call the attempt to link random events with our own thought processes the "illusion of control." Dr. [Susan] Blackmore gives a simple example that we have all experienced—willing traffic lights to change as we approach them. If the lights do change we get a pleasant lift, but people often report such coincidental events as evidence of psychokinesis, or mind over matter. In other words, physical objects have somehow reordered themselves in accordance with a thought in someone's mind. Investigations have revealed that people who report such powers routinely ignore those occasions when the lights do not change, if they notice them at all.

"We like to think we can control the world around us by observing coincidences between our own actions and the things that happen," says Dr. Blackmore. "Belief in psychic events may be an illusion of causality."

Psychics respond to such criticisms by asserting that human intuition is a greater force than science allows, yet altogether too subtle and idiosyncratic to be subjected to the empirical tests that science demands. "We are more powerful than we know," says Craig Hamilton Parker, who describes himself as a psychic. "In my work as a medium I have found the spiritual state of people influences the world around them. We can change events with the power of thought. Mind can influence matter. With training we can make our own world and the whole world better."

He says there is no such thing as chance, merely human will. "Coincidences are nothing of the sort, just our awareness that the outer world is actually an inner world. Coincidences synchronize the inner and the outer worlds."

Periodical Bibliography

The following articles have been selected to supplement the diverse views presented in this chapter.

Stephen Armstrong "Generation X-Files: The Psychic Schools Have Never Been So Busy, and It's Not the Doris Stokes Brigade Who Want to Learn, but the Young, the Prosperous and the Educated," *New Statesman (1996)*, August 7, 2006.

Jesse M. Bering "The Cognitive Psychology of Belief in the Supernatural: Belief in a Deity or an Afterlife Could Be an Evolutionarily Advantageous By-Product of People's Ability to Reason about the Minds of Others," *American Scientist*, March-April 2006.

Deepak Chopra and Michael Shermer "The Value of Skepticism: Is Skepticism a Negative or Positive for Science and Humanity?" *eSkpetic*, September 28, 2005.

Daniel Kinsman "How to Be a Nice Skeptic," http://kinsman.is-a-geek.net/blog, October 3, 2007.

Sverre Pettersen and Rolf V. Olsen "Exploring Predictors of Health Sciences Students' Attitudes towards Complementary-Alternative Medicine," *Advances in Health Sciences Education*, February 2007.

Matthew J. Sharps, Justin Matthews, and Jane Asten "Cognition and Belief in Paranormal Phenomena: Gestalt/Feature-Intensive Processing Theory and Tendencies toward ADHD, Depression, and Dissociation," *Journal of Psychology*, November 2006.

D. L. Stewart "Sometimes Even a Skeptic Has to Wonder," *Dayton Daily News*, October 7, 2007.

Emyr Williams, Leslie J. Francis, and Mandy Robbins "Personality and Paranormal Belief: A Study among Adolescents," *Pastoral Psychology*, September 2007.

Thomas de Zengotita "Believing Whatever," *Chronicle of Higher Education*, November 11, 2005.

OPPOSING
VIEWPOINTS®
SERIES

CHAPTER 2

Do Paranormal Phenomena Exist?

Chapter Preface

Scientists do not know everything, but they have figured out an awful lot. So much, in fact, that some of them seem to behave as if everything knowable has already been discovered. In contrast to this general attitude of skepticism is an unabashed excitement about what could be lurking around the corner. Occupying the murky space in between these two extremes of thought are both the next scientific breakthrough and whimsical imagination.

Germ theory, the telephone, incandescent light bulbs, and even airplanes are all legitimate scientific discoveries that were initially rejected or ridiculed by established and respected scientists. In fact, even though there were photographs and eyewitness accounts of Orville and Wilbur Wright's airplane flying, newspapers and journals dismissed the evidence out of hand. One newspaper, the Paris edition of the *Herald Tribune*, suggested that they were lying about their achievements!

Obviously, heavier-than-air flight is not a paranormal phenomenon—the global community is a testament to that. Airplanes and spacecraft technologies have proliferated as a result of the intensive scientific research into the physics of flight that was conducted after two bicycle manufacturers—with a vision—proved that man-directed flight was possible. The idea that someone could fly moved from the realm of the paranormal into the realm of normal. At any moment, some other equally unexpected concept could do the same thing.

Researchers of subjects currently considered paranormal are as sincere about their experiments' potential as were the Wright brothers. For every paranormal researcher who is a scientific hobbyist, there is another one who is a credentialed academic with publications in peer-reviewed journals. For every outlandish claim contested by the scientific establishment, there is an accepted outlandish claim so arcane that only a handful of people have the knowledge to understand it (like some of the theories in quantum physics). On the other hand, for every scientist accused of being too stubborn to accept a new idea, there is another scientist too enthusiastic about an early experimental result that has yet to be replicated in another laboratory.

If the history of scientific exploration has taught one thing, it is that even the most informed people can be proven wrong—accepted theories about the world and the universe are supplanted by new ones on a regular basis. It is usually not until one creative person demonstrates the impossible to be possible that anyone else thinks about it in the first place! Some future commonplace technology or ability could seem like magic to people today.

The following chapter explores the boundaries of what is known about the world and what can be reasonably predicted about what is unknown, and how data from paranormal experiments are to be interpreted.

> "When Uri Geller said to go find a broken watch, I remembered one we had in this 'junk' drawer. I pulled on the drawer and there it was: ticking away!"

Observers Have Witnessed Psychokinesis

Doug Yurchey

Doug Yurchey has studied ancient mysteries for more than thirty years. He has lectured at Carnegie Mellon University and California State University at Northridge. The following viewpoint describes the psychokinetic/telekinetic abilities (using the mind to move matter) of Uri Geller, a man who became famous in the 1970s for using his mind to bend spoons. Yurchey shares the story of the broken watch that made him a believer in Geller's talent. Yurchey points out that the "Geller Effect" only works when Geller is surrounded by the positive energy that believers generate. He also remarks that he has not personally experienced the Geller Effect since divorcing his wife, who is psychic.

As you read, consider the following questions:

1. On what information does the author of this viewpoint base his opinion about Uri Geller's psychokinetic abilities?

Doug Yurchey, "My Experience with Uri Geller," www.world-mysteries.com, 2002. Reproduced by permission.

2. What conclusion does the author want readers to draw about Geller's radio appearances and the manifestation of the Star of David?

3. How does the author interpret Geller's refusal to interact with him on stage during the June 1976 performance?

In the 1970s, Uri Geller became a controversial personality, appearing on television, radio and giving many public performances. The Israeli psychic could bend spoons, start broken watches and move objects with his mind. This immediately began a firestorm between believers and nonbelievers. Is he a fraud and a con artist? Or, does he actually have extraordinary abilities? . . .

Skeptics came out of the woodwork and attacked Uri Geller. The psychic divided America as well as the rest of the world. There are positive people who are open-minded and there are negative people who love to criticize. A war began between Uri Geller and the magicians. These magicians (who truly are con men, deceivers and tricksters) would not accept the fact that someone really had phenomenal abilities. It must be a trick; it could not possibly be real. . . .

Geller's abilities have been *proven* by Stanford Research Institute, UCLA, Kent State, Birbeck College University of London, Foch Hospital Lab in France, Lawrence Livermore Radiation Labs, U.S. Naval Ordinance Labs and other prestigious institutions. That is not why I believe in Uri Geller. I can speak with certainty because of a few "personal experiences" which are the best teachers of all.

Bending Metal

I came home from work one day to discover my wife (who was psychic and now an ex-wife) in an excited state about who was on television. It was this psychic, who we had never heard of, performing on the *Mike Douglas Show*. I sat down and was instantly intrigued. When Uri Geller said to go find a broken watch, I remembered one we had in this "junk" drawer. I pulled on the drawer and there it was: ticking away! This was very strange because the last hundred times I opened it, the watch remained broken. I don't know why it wasn't thrown away. Why was this time, when we attempted to mentally start the watch, the one time where it worked perfectly? Television stations would be flooded with phone calls because of Geller. The phenomena actually happened in people's homes when Uri made television appearances.

The first time there was any metal-bending in our apartment was when Kathy wrote a letter to Uri Geller. The metal clip on her Flair pen slowly curled up as she wrote the letter! This began many strange instances of the Geller Effect. In front of me now, as I write this article, I've placed an old box of bent silverware/keys/etc. from that time period. This box of memories I cherish. There is a story behind each item:

- There are 8 Flair pens with their pocket clips in various positions up to 90 degrees; 2 have broken off completely.

- There is a set of 10 keys and 8 of them are bent.

- 7 spoons and 2 forks are bent.

- A thick, kitchen drawer handle is very bent.

- Something sliced through a large pair of metal scissors chopping off the ends. The cuts, an inch and a half from the tips, are smooth, not jagged.

- A sample, metal, Social Security card is warped.

- There is also a broken off television antenna.

The antenna is an odd story. We woke up one morning to find both of our TV aerials bent almost 90 degrees like floppy, rabbit ears. I was half asleep and began to rebend one of the antennas back into position. Well, you can't physically bend a TV antenna. It broke off in my hand. Kathy got worried and became very upset. She was thinking that this power was destructive. When we came back into the room, we were startled to see that the remaining antenna had straightened all by itself! There it stood; a TV with a straight antenna and the other broken off. We took this as a sign that everything was all right. This thing that was happening, whatever it was, was not from a destructive source . . . but a positive one.

We would often open our silverware drawer and discover that half of the utensils were bent. We would have to rebend our silverware just so we could eat! Kathy and I would have to explain to dinner guests why there were kinks in our utensils.

A Personal Encounter

On 5/5/76, Geller appeared on a local, live television program in Pittsburgh called the *Marie Torre Show*. Uri was given an envelope and was asked what was inside. Geller got it wrong. He said: Is someone thinking Star of David? In our living room, Kathy was holding a Star of David pendant at that same moment. Later, the same day, Geller was on the *Roy Fox Show* on KDKA radio. Something compelled Kathy to tune in. She called and called to try to get through and speak to Geller. On the phone, she told Uri that she was the one thinking Star of David earlier that day. Uri turned to the radio host and said: "I don't know this woman. I didn't tell her to call at this time." You see . . . Geller had been doodling, on a pad, the Star of David.

Later, Kathy called hotel after hotel trying to find where Uri was staying. I got a ride from a friend and we headed off to a Marriott Inn. We stayed there for quite a while looking for Uri Geller. It was like a needle in a haystack.

But, the way this day had been going, (it was my 25th birthday) I had a good feeling we would run into him. And, we did. Uri and his friend, Shipi Shtrang, passed us in the hall. They had gone to a Pirates baseball game. I introduced myself [and said] that it was my wife with the Star of David.

Conrad's Human Telekinesis Equation

$$TK = CFe + VC + ZPE - SD - E+$$

Wherein:

TK is Telekinesis. The ability to cause at a distance by cerebral-generated motive power the movement of matter or energy. . . .

CFe is Cerebro Iron. Sufficient circulating iron in the brain and stored iron in the skull's bone marrow. . . .

VC is Visual Contact. The target must be visually sighted in sufficient lighting with open space along the pathway in front of it. Repeated experiments . . . found that closing one's eyes or attempting telekinesis in a darkened room produced negative results. . . .

ZPE is Zero Point Emotions. No willpower or imagination is involved, both of which consume brain energy.

SD is No Sleep Deprivation, which inhibits mental functioning.

E+ is No excessive level of vitamin E in the body. Vitamin E systemically protects the body from excess iron and can make it difficult to absorb and raise iron levels.

James A. Conrad, "Telekinesis Equation Revealed," www.mindpowernews.com, 2007. Reproduced by permission.

He invited us into his hotel room where we talked for nearly an hour. I remember I had more to say about aliens than he did . . . also, he was impressed when I showed him a photo of our baby, Rose.

Geller wrote free passes to a performance he was giving [the] next month at Pittsburgh's Soldiers & Sailors Auditorium. Geller wanted to give us a souvenir and offered to bend one of our keys. But, the only key we had was my friend's car key. We couldn't get home if he bent that. . .so Uri took his Marriott room key and began gently stroking it. This was not planned; it was spontaneous; it was done a foot from my face and it certainly *bent*. We were believers. There was no negativity in the air. The key, room 620, began warping within seconds. It was a moment I'll never forget.

The Geller Effect

On 6/18/76, myself and Kathy attended Uri's performance. We got word to him that I had a drawing that I wanted Uri to see. His "act" was mind-blowing and he beat the odds in many respects. There was a point when Uri asked the audience if your keys have bent or watches have begun to work, please come forward to the stage. Our spoons and keys bent as well as the thick kitchen drawer handle. I marched forward and was a little surprised that it didn't happen to everyone. About 5% of the crowd experienced the Geller Effect. But, as soon as Uri saw me, he said: "No. Not you. I don't want to deal with you." I was shocked as I made my way back to my seat.

Kathy and I figured that Uri only wanted to work with people he had never seen. Someone may have seen us together at the Marriott and thought we had this planned. This tells me that the man has integrity. Kathy and I were able to talk to him on stage after everyone had gone. Shipi took photographs of us and he liked my drawing.

Another strange thing occurred a few months later. *ESP Magazine* ran a front cover with bold letters: On Sept. 1, 1976 AT 11 PM E.D.T. THIS COVER CAN BEND YOUR KEYS. This truly was a happening with Uri Geller (and anyone who wanted to participate) concentrating at this specific time. The public was to place their keys, spoons and broken watches on the magazine and see if the focused energy would have any effect. Also, a 2-digit number was going to be transmitted and people were to see if they could accurately receive it. Again, our spoons bent, but not very much. What I remember is: We had a broken air-pump on our aquarium. I placed it on the *ESP* issue at the appropriate moment. We concentrated. I hooked it back up to the tank. The pump worked so strongly; it was like there was nothing wrong with it. We did receive the 2-digit number correctly: it was 42.

On 10/7/76 . . . Kathy, myself and a friend named Bruce all concentrated to again generate this unusual ability. We sat cross-legged on our living room floor with our hands about a foot over a spoon. (Most of the utensil-bending, I admit, I did not directly observe. Rather, we found them that way in the silverware drawer). On this occasion, we witnessed the spoon bend in less than a minute. It could not bend any more. The handle touched the scoop part of the spoon. How does an *untouched* spoon decide to curl up in 30 seconds? I know this because I labeled the spoon: 10/7/76 with Bruce. I would be very upset if someone took a spoon from my box of special bent stuff and physically changed their shape. I want them in the shape they are in because I know that they were not physically bent.

Kathy and I divorced in 1977 and the Geller Effect has not happened around me since way back then. . . . Often public opinion is nowhere near the truth. Do not be swayed by skeptical people. I would rather know the truth and be in the unpopular minority than go along with the crowd and be so far away from the truth.

On a *Where Are They Now?* [television] episode, I found out that Geller has been very successful finding (dowsing) oil, gold and water for big companies. No one is going to pay large sums of money unless they are convinced that their source of information is legitimate.

> *"Nobody has been able to prove ghosts don't exist, but science has proven that they can't act the way they do."*

Ghosts Are Incompatible with Scientific Principles

Lucian Dorneanu

Lucian Dorneanu is a Science Editor at Softpedia, an online library of technological and scientific information. He makes no claims in about the existence of ghosts, but he does provide scientific reasons for why ghosts—beings consisting entirely of energy and not matter—could not walk, chill the air, speak, or even be seen. Basic laws and principles of physics prevent it. As you read the following viewpoint, consider the ghostly behaviors reported by people who believe in them. Why do believers attribute these abilities to ghosts?

As you read, consider the following questions:

1. Why does it matter if a ghost is made of matter or of energy?

2. What are two physical characteristics of sound that the author uses to support his argument?

Lucian Dorneanu, "Why Ghosts Can't Walk Through Walls . . . and More—Scientific Arguments," *Softpedia News*, 2007. Reproduced by permission.

3. Why does the author make a distinction between whether or not ghosts exist and whether or not ghosts behave as portrayed in the culture?

Hollywood movies are full of monsters, bad guys, aliens and mythological creatures, which make the good guys look better after saving the world, or at least some damsel in distress. While some depictions are scientifically documented, some of them are just plain impossible and could only exist in people's imagination.

Science laws debunk many of these myths and prove that they simply can't exist in the physical world, as we know it. So let's look at one example of "beings that can not be."

The ghost is thought to be the apparition of a deceased person, frequently similar in appearance to that person, and encountered in places he or she frequented, or in association with the person's former belongings. It also often refers to the souls, of spirits of those who can't find eternal rest and wander the world in search of resolution.

Walking Through Walls

Nobody has been able to prove ghosts don't exist, but science has proven that they can't act the way they do. For instance, their ability to walk through walls is a common talent of Hollywood ghosts. There's one problem here. Newton's laws of physics say that if a ghost can walk, it shouldn't be able to pass through walls, since a body at rest will remain so until it's subjected to an external force and for every action there is an equal but opposite reaction.

This is exactly the case with walking ghosts. If it walks, it must by applying a force to the ground it steps on and the ground must apply to the ghost an equal and opposite force, that pushes the body forward. This means that a ghost must be made of matter, and not energy.

Supposing it's made of energy could explain the fact that ghosts may pass through walls, but most certainly, they couldn't walk. And if a ghost could walk through walls, this means it could also pass through the floor. If a ghost were able to stay on the floor without passing through it, then it would have to apply a force to the floor, whose equal reaction should keep her on the floor. Pure energy couldn't do that.

Chill Effect

Another ghost myth says that sharp drops in temperature are also associated with the arrival of a spiritual presence.

It has become almost a Hollywood cliché that the entrance of a ghostly presence is foreshadowed by a sudden and overwhelming chill. Again physics says it's not possible, or at least that ghosts can't be responsible for such a phenomenon.

In fact, when a warm object is placed next to a cold object, energy flows from the warm body to the cooler body, cooling the warm body. So if a ghost causes the air in a room to cool down, that means the original heat of the air must transfer onto a cooler body, which rapidly warms up.

It seems that when a ghost causes the temperature in a room to drop, the ghost itself warms up, so all ghosts should be hot. But if ghosts are made of pure energy, where did the warmth go? Energy doesn't just heat up, like matter.

Again, if ghosts were made of matter, they could absorb the thermal energy of the surrounding air, becoming hot themselves, but they won't be able to pass through walls, so they must enter and leave through a door or window.

A more likely explanation for the chilling effect would be a sudden draft, occurring in a room with a high window or a door with a gap, where the cool air from outside displaces warm air inside, creating a system of heat cycles and eddies. This creates a combination of air currents that may cause temperatures to drop up to 2°C, and the effect would be increased by the fact that humans are more sensitive to rapid changes in temperature even if the absolute change is small.

Joe Nickell Investigates a "Haunted" House

I found a caretaker next door who had asked me in a cagey fashion did I believe in ghosts, did I want to see a ghost, and if I'd come back that evening he would personally show me the ghosts—his eyes twinkling. When I went back that evening, he showed me the staircase and told me about late-night clean-up crews, or family members going up and down the stairs— which, in his opinion, was almost certainly the source of the ghostly footfalls. If you were in the far bedroom in the McKenzie House, indeed you would hear "way over there" footsteps on the stairs, and in fact they were mere inches away from the stairs you had in mind. . . .

The ghostly phenomena, I believe, came from the McMillan building next door. The caretaker told me that one night he heard some sounds in the back and investigated, and discovered some college boys had a listening device hooked up to the back of the house, some earphones, and they were hearing various "ghostly" noises. They let him have a listen, and after a minute or so he handed the earphones back and told them "Well, boys, I hate to tell you, but the sounds you're hearing are caused by the automatic flush on the men's urinal next door."

This had been a lesson for me, because these phenomena had gone on for some ten years, and when I asked the caretaker why he hadn't come forward, because he had been chuckling to himself off and on, he told me that he had made up his mind that if anyone ever asked him outright he would—but no one ever had! I was amazed that no one—none of the ghost hunters, journalists, exorcists, nobody had ever spent the night in the house, or conducted an exorcism. Nobody. Not one. And nobody had ever bothered to go next door, to a building not 40 inches away.

John C. Snider, "The Joe Nickell Files: Hauntings," 2004.
www.scifidimensions.com.

Sounds

Another phenomenon associated with ghosts is the sound. Most ghosts in alleged sightings are not talking, but some of them are, even though this is not possible. Speech can be described as an act of producing voice through the use of the vocal folds and vocal apparatus to create a linguistic act designed to convey information.

Speech involves air, and air can't be manipulated into forming recognizable sounds by a ghost who's made of energy. So ghosts can't talk. Some of you would say that maybe the ghost is able to communicate through telepathy. That hasn't been proven so far, but supposing they posses this form of communication, why don't all of them talk?

A possible explanation for the ghosts is in fact related to sounds. Frequencies lower than 20 hertz are called infrasound and are normally inaudible, but British scientists Richard Lord and Richard Wiseman have concluded that infrasound can cause humans to feel a "presence" in the room, or unexplained feelings of anxiety or dread. . . .

Sight

The last, and probably the most important with ghosts is that we shouldn't be able to see them. Why? Because the sight is the ability to interpret visible light information reaching the eyes, after it bounces off a surface.

How can light bounce off an inexistent surface, when ghosts are made of energy?

Although the physical arguments present above do not deny the existence of ghosts, I hope that they made you at least ask yourself some questions, before believing everything Hollywood is shoving down our throat.

> *"The most extraordinary thing about the ancient world's binary soul doctrine is that it seems consistent with the latest findings in a number of areas of modern scientific research."*

Ghosts Are Compatible with Scientific Principles

Peter Novak

Peter Novak is a former psychological counselor who has spent nearly twenty years researching cultural legends and reports of life after death. He is particularly interested in the duality of the human brain (with its two hemispheres) and has appeared on many talk shows and at conferences in North America and Europe. The following viewpoint addresses the similarities between ancient beliefs about the two parts of the soul and modern scientific findings about the brain. Novak says that reports about the behavior and appearance of ghosts are consistent with the "Binary Soul Doctrine" and theories in psychology about right brain and left brain thought patterns.

As you read, consider the following questions:

1. What behaviors do "tapeloop" ghosts and Alzheimer's patients have in common?

Peter Novak, "Ghosts, Poltergeists, and the Lost Secret of Death," *Ghost! Magazine*, 2006. Reproduced by permission of the author.

2. What "right brain" behaviors are exhibited when ghosts try to communicate with living people?

3. Why does the author describe poltergeists as having a conscious (rather than unconscious) mind?

People all across the globe once believed virtually the same thing about what happened after death—that human beings possess not one, but two souls, which were in danger of dividing apart from one another when a person died.

After leaving the physical body, one of these souls was often expected to reincarnate, while the other was believed to become trapped in a dreamlike netherworld. Some of these cultures believed that the after-death division of these two souls could be prevented or reversed, while others saw the division as being inevitable and permanent.

The most extraordinary thing about the ancient world's binary soul doctrine [BSD] is that it seems consistent with the latest findings in a number of areas of modern scientific research. For one thing, these cultures' descriptions of the two souls are strikingly similar to modern science's "right brain/ left brain" descriptions of the conscious and unconscious halves of the human psyche. . . .

If the conscious and unconscious halves of the human psyche were to divide apart at death, virtually all modern and classic descriptions of afterlife phenomena would be explained.

"Tapeloop" Ghosts

Modern reports of ghosts and poltergeists fall right in line with the expectations of the BSD. The vast majority of haunting ghosts go through the same motions again and again, virtually oblivious to the presence of the living. Each time they appear, these specters look the same, wearing the same period clothing and hairstyles, often standing in the exact same spot or traveling along the same route. In buildings whose floor plans were changed at some point in their past, ghosts are sometimes observed moving along those previous floor plans, traveling through doorways or along staircases that no longer exist. . . .

For nearly a century, many ghost researchers have concurred that these "tapeloop" ghosts were not really souls of the dead at all, but just some bit of discarded psychic rubbish left by the soul's passing into the next world. However, modern research into Alzheimer's disease has raised some doubt about this time-worn conclusion. The behavior of Alzheimer's patients seems to have a great deal in common with the behavior reported about these sort of ghosts. It is also very common for Alzheimer's patients to wander mindlessly through their old behavior patterns, endlessly repeating old, habitual actions for no apparent reason. When they are in the middle of such "spells", they don't seem to realize that they are lost, they don't respond when addressed, and they seldom seek help on their own. These multiple parallels are suggesting to some modern ghost researchers that these tapeloop ghosts may not be empty images after all, but the mentally ill (i.e., mentally dysfunctional) souls of the dead.

Right-Brain Behaviors

Despite the sounds that sometimes accompany hauntings, when these ghosts visibly appear they are usually completely silent and almost never verbalize any intelligible speech. The vast majority of ghosts make no attempt to communicate with others, acting as if they are entirely unaware of the presence of the living. And when communication is received from ghosts, it is almost always entirely subjective in nature, using gestures, signals, images, and symbols—classic right-brain formatting of information. There is a very long history of the non-verbal nature of these entities; even the souls of the dead in Homer's *Iliad* are portrayed as being unable to speak properly. Haunting ghosts virtually never use left-brain commun-ication techniques such as codes or spoken or written lan-guage, or any sort of linear message format.

While the average person usually can't communicate with ghosts at all, some psychics maintain they can. In fact, psy-chics tend to divide haunting ghosts into two groups—those they can communicate with, and those they can't. Those they can't, psychics often claim, are not real beings at all, but merely non-sentient memory recordings. But to the average person, these two categories of ghosts seem indistinguishable—both appear at the same place every time they are seen, always wearing the same thing and doing the same thing, both seem-ing equally caught up in their emotional memories, attitudes, and behaviors from the past. It seems unlikely that two en-tirely separate kinds of phenomena could look and behave so much the same. The binary soul doctrine, of course, would suggest that both categories are living sentient beings, but the non-communicative ones are functioning more exclusively through the right-brain unconscious half of their minds, which would cause them to have less objective awareness and be less able to interact with others. Such ghosts would be quite like a comatose patient—still alive, but imprisoned in-side their own unconscious.

Many ghosts are reported to have haunted the same loca-tions for 200 years or more, apparently never realizing that they are dead or that time has moved on. This suggests, of course, that somehow they've lost the ability to make even the most elementary logical deductions. Ghosts can apparently have the most obvious clues staring them right in the face for centuries, watching their hands, legs, and bodies pass thru solid objects, without it ever crossing their mind that they might have died. These haunting ghosts just can't seem to fig-ure this out on their own, exactly as if they'd lost their own logical and analytical intellect. . . .

Do Ghosts Possess Intelligence?
An Answer from India's Traditions

The intellect of normal human beings is directed towards accomplishing various tasks in the world to satisfy them at a physical, psychological and spiritual level. The human intellect has an inherent discriminatory element that guides the person about what is right and what is wrong, also what is to be pursued and what is to be abandoned.

When we pass on and if we become ghosts, we tend to lose this discriminatory intelligence. The reason for this is that as subtle bodies, the main body is the mental body, which is full of desires. The intellect is then used single-mindedly to fulfill these desires. This is unlike on Earth where the intellect is used for a variety of things, physical activity included such as earning a living, etc.

As a ghost becomes obsessed with fulfilling their desires or troubling others, their intellect is directed completely in this direction itself. The intellect is totally ego-based and restricted to acquiring power.

Spiritual Science Research Foundation,
"Different Features of Ghosts," Spiritual Causes of Difficulties, 2007.
www.spiritualresearchfoundation.org.

Left-Brain Behavior

The poltergeist seems an equal-but-opposite version of a haunting ghost. While ghosts are more frequently seen than heard, poltergeists are more commonly heard than seen. People often mention how strangely quiet the air seems to get when a ghost appears; and when a ghost does make audible sounds, they are usually nonverbal whistles, chirps, screams, or moans, all of which are subjective right-brain sounds that need to be interpreted by the listener. The poltergeist, on the other hand, seems to be more of a no-nonsense left-brain communicator; many have been known to employ a sophisticated linear communication code consisting of knocks, raps, and scratches, and a number have even been known to use language, sometimes speaking and occasionally even using the written word. While haunting ghosts' communication attempts are usually limited to nonverbal signals, gestures, and images, poltergeists virtually never resort to symbol or metaphor to get their messages across; they're just not that subtle.

Whereas the haunting ghost seems to be caught up in their own subjective memories and emotional turmoil, the poltergeist usually seems quite objective, extroverted, and other-oriented, not particularly interested in its own memories or emotions at all, but very attentive to the memories, emotions, and reactions of others. While most haunting ghosts never notice the presence of others, poltergeists always seem to be aware of what's going on around them in the real world. While the haunting ghost is known for its fixed and consistent behavior, poltergeists are known for being unpredictable and inconstant.

Ghosts tend to be seen again and again at the same place, doing the same thing in the same clothes; many even adhere to a specific timetable, appearing at regular intervals, or on the same anniversary date year after year. But poltergeist manifestations tend to be erratic, appearing suddenly, carrying on for anywhere from a few weeks to a year or two, and then inexplicably stop just as suddenly, usually never resuming again. Poltergeists, in short, seem to exhibit much more free will than the typical haunting ghost does, and that is exactly what the BSD would predict, as free will is exercised by the conscious mind, not the unconscious.

Clues to the poltergeist's nature and identity are usually absent. While a haunting ghost gives every indication of having a clear and definite identity, poltergeists often seem to have no clear identity of their own, sometimes presenting no identity at all, and other times offering a variety of different, mutually exclusive identities. In one study, more than 80% of poltergeists did not present any clear personal identity. This too is exactly what one would expect from a separated conscious mind; without the unconscious, it would have no memory.

This, of course, is all exactly what one would expect from a disembodied conscious mind that had lost its unconscious. Just as the behavior of haunting ghosts matches up perfectly with the BSD's expectations for a disembodied unconscious mind with no conscious, so too the behavior of poltergeists matches the BSD's expectations for a disembodied conscious mind with no unconscious.

> *"There's never been a time where there's been a buyer's—and seller's—market like there is now."*

Psychics Are Frauds

Janet McDonald

Janet McDonald, the author of young adult novels, saw the psychic Sylvia Browne on a television interview show. Impressed by how callers to the program responded to Browne's predictions and readings, McDonald decided to purchase her services for help exploring some of the questions that had troubled her. The following viewpoint describes her conversation with the psychic and her own reactions to the information she is given. As you read, consider McDonald's suspicions about how Browne came up with the predictions she made.

As you read, consider the following questions:

1. What suggests to the author that the psychic might be authentic?

2. Why does the author resist the urge to respond to the psychic's comments about her personal life?

Janet McDonald, "Crystal Bawl: I Blew $700 on a Psychic Whose Best Talent Was Predicting My Gullibility," Salon.com, January 8, 2003. This article first appeared in Salon-.com, at http://www.salon.com. An online version remains in the Salon archives. Reprinted with permission.

3. Why doesn't the psychic's corporation guarantee customer satisfaction or give refunds?

Despite what you're about to read, I am arguably not a complete idiot.

I have degrees from three Ivy League schools in French literature, journalism and law. I've authored books. Three of them, to be exact. OK, so they're not *Anna Karenina* or *The Bluest Eye* or *The Years* but still, they're published and are on display atop my mother's dresser drawer, between the Eiffel Tower snow globe and the photo of me grinning next to a life-size cardboard replica of Bill Clinton.

And I'm not some gullible white-bread girl from Kansas. I'm streetwise, born and bred in a Brooklyn housing project.

So I wonder, how did an aging and undoubtedly bleached blonde with a crystal ball and the smoky voice of a barroom broad make a loser of a lawyer and a punk of a project girl— and walk off with 700 of my hard-earned dollars?

I know exactly what went wrong; I'm an idiot.

An Astounding Performance

My first error was to mistake CNN's Larry King for a journalist. King's universe of newsworthy interviewees consists mostly of actresses and babes who look like actresses, real actors and hunky inspirational speakers who look like actors, and real models and disfigured beauties made to look, after expensive reconstructive surgery, like models. And there are the famous psychics.

My second error was to jot down the name of famous psychic and regular "Larry King Live" guest Sylvia Browne, as I watched her perform. I don't believe in psychics. Really. But I was impressed by this one. I got chills watching her, hearing the gasps, squeals and sobs of callers as she shocked and comforted them with precise descriptions of their dearly departed loved ones. I'd seen Sylvia Browne solve mysteries and identify callers' spirit guides and guardian angels, and confidently assure everyone that spouse, lover, dad, mom, son, daughter, sister, brother, grandparent, poodle was in heaven and doing great.

Something made me believe against reason that Sylvia Browne might give me the answers to questions that were troubling me. How could Sept. 11 have happened? Should I stay in Paris or move to New York, which in its sudden noble vulnerability seemed to be calling me home? Should I continue practicing law or would my fledgling writing career save me from a life of contract-churning drudgery?

With a mixture of curiosity, hope and embarrassment I went to Browne's Web site, read up on the famous psychic and swallowed so hard at the cost of a reading that I nearly choked ($750 for an in-person reading with Sylvia; those on a tight budget could consult her by telephone for $700 or talk with her presumably half-gifted son for half-price, $350). I made an appointment to have a telephone consultation, for which I had to pay in advance by credit card.

Then I was dogged by doubts and miserly misgivings, exacerbated by the reactions of friends, a group of overeducated, unevolved cynics with faint, dingy auras. They laughed at my enthusiasm for the famous psychic and even questioned the origin of the phone calls to the King show, smirking that the callers all seemed to be women from somewhere in Nova Scotia. But it's CNN, I protested, and they'd check for that kind of thing. Right?

"Omigod! Omigod! How'd you know that?" callers enthused.

"Honey, I'm a psychic," she'd answer time and again in that gravelly, cocky voice. I was taken. And how.

First Impressions

I'd been told the night before by Browne's corporation scheduler that Sylvia would call, tell me spontaneously about myself

What Do You Consider a "Really Long Life"?

Young adult author Janet McDonald, a prominent voice who reached African-American teens who felt underrepresented in books, died of cancer in Paris on April 11. She was 53.

Debra Lau Whelan,
"Young Adult Author Janet McDonald Dies at 53,"
School Library Journal, *April 16, 2007.*

and my life, and then respond to questions. So I was sitting by the phone with my list of questions, sweating with anticipation, when the phone rang. On the other end was The Voice.

"I discovered you on 'Larry King Live' two years ago," I said breathlessly.

"Oh yeah, I've been on there five, six times. Janet, how are you doing with headaches and stomach and lower back?"

I rarely get headaches, have a steel trap for a stomach and go to the gym several times a week. But I searched for something, eager to get my reading off to a good start.

"Umm, OK, I had been having lower back pain, um . . . in the past."

"I'd start doing some stomach crunches on the bed. Then I would really start trying to take some lecithin."

"OK," I said, writing down my instructions. It occurred to me that in our high-stress, sedentary world most people had headaches, stomachaches and lower back pain. But she was probably warming up before zeroing in on me specifically.

"L-E-C-I-T-H-I-N," said the psychic.

Why was she spelling it? Didn't she know that I was a spelling champion all through school?

She went on generically about protein and blood sugar and fatigue. I stared at the clock and my list of questions. She suggested I eat chicken and fish. I already did, and often.

Then she hit me with her psychic beam: "You're an activator and a catalyst and people like you need to have two or three things on the burner."

"It can get problematical in relationships," I said. Relationships. We were on our way. My money was being well spent, after all.

Helping the Psychic

"Oh yeah, but not if you meet someone who's strong enough to handle it. Did you ever notice in the world people don't take well to strong women? We're all for strong men but when a woman gets strong everybody gets nervous.

A strong man? There weren't any men in my life. But I resisted the urge to speak, not wanting to give her cues or prompts.

"You have had kind of an alone time, but that's all right."

Alone? I hadn't been single for years. My neck began to tense. Maybe if I just gave her a little nudge in the right direction . . . So I said I was conflicted about moving back to New York.

"I think it's time to go back to New York. Let's say that's where your fortune lies. But it does look like you're gonna get . . . I don't want to call it a sideline, but you're gonna get into buying real estate and investing in real estate."

"Really?" I was puzzled. A born renter, I have never in my life owned a co-op, a condo, a house or even an empty lot.

"You can't go wrong, especially in the States where there's never been a time where there's been a buyer's—and seller's—market like there is now. I mean, you could buy something in Podunk, Idaho, and it's good."

What was she talking about?! This was my $700 reading? My stomach hurt. She hadn't been like this on "Larry King Live." She'd made sense. She knew what dead people looked like.

Past Lives and Spirit Guides

I gave her one more chance. I asked about Sept. 11.

"Well, honey, I think everybody took a hit on that one. I don't care where . . . they could be in outer Mongolia . . . and I think it's not just the World Trade Center; I think it's just . . . everything . . . went . . . goofy."

Goofy?! I cast desperately for a topic that might offer some success. I asked again about relationships. She asked who was "the darker-haired one"? Hellooo! Surely she knew I'm black. Surely she knew that means almost everyone in my life has dark hair.

What about the spirit guides and angels she and Larry King had discussed?

"You have, uh, four, uh, angels, and a very, very strong male guide by the name of Khalib."

"And the angels?"

"Just angels."

"Male or female?"

"They're androgynous," she said with what I thought was a touch of impatience.

I always wanted a twin. What the hell, might as well ask her about that, too.

"You had one in a past life . . . a hundred years ago . . . in France. A twin sister. You two were inseparable and had a mil-linery shop in Versailles."

Black twins with a hat store in the King's court. Right.

I was screwed. I had thrown away in a half-hour more money than my poor project mother collects from Social Se-curity in a month.

I wrapped it up with a question about my longevity.

"Oh, God, yes, a really long life," said the All-Seeing One. "And thank God you won't be stupid or incapacitated. I don't mind living to be old as long as I'm not an idiot."

No danger there, Sylvia. I'm the idiot.

A few weeks later I requested a refund and was sent a standard Refund Policy letter: "The services provided by Sylvia Browne Corporation are highly speculative in nature and we do not guarantee that the results of our work will be satisfactory to a client."

Now that's psychic.

> "There was an instant connection. McKoy sensed things about Augie that only Tabatha knew."

Psychics Have Real Ability

Doug Moe

Doug Moe is a daily columnist for The Capital Times *and the former editor of* Madison Magazine. *Although he is well known for his ability to find a compelling story in ordinary events, the following viewpoint tells the extraordinary tale of a puppy lost in a storm and the psychic who predicted the circumstances of its return to its owners. The story is presented chronologically. As you read, compare what the psychic predicts to the events that unfold.*

As you read, consider the following questions:

1. Why does Karla McKoy say that animal communication is not an "exact science"?
2. What predictions did McKoy make about the missing puppy?
3. What circumstances surrounding this case suggest that McKoy is an authentic psychic?

This story involves a Wisconsin blizzard, an Illinois pet psychic and a private investigator from Portland, Ore., catching a midnight flight to Madison to find a missing dog.

What more do you want? A happy ending? Read on.

One of the strange things about last month's snowstorm was the thunder. Thursday morning, Feb. 16, the snow was relentless. But while the temperature would plummet on the heels of the storm, that morning the air was mild enough to bring lightning and thunder along with the snowfall.

It was surreal, but for Tabatha Bell it was worse than that. It was the thunder that made Augie run away.

"We were in Cam-Rock Park." Bell, was saying Thursday. The park is near the Cambridge home that Bell shares with her husband, John Bell, and Augie, a 7-month-old sheltie puppy.

It was about 9 a.m. when the first crack of thunder sent Augie scampering back toward where Tabatha had parked her car. Bell, following, realized it might be a good idea to be getting home.

Then there was another crack of thunder, and Augie—who at 7 months had not heard a lot of booms from the sky—took off for the wooded wetlands that surround the park.

Disappearing into the Storm

Bell gave chase, and for a time the fresh snow made the dog's prints easier to follow. But it soon became clear that Augie had become confused—the paw prints began going in circles—and Bell, frustrated by the snow—"I couldn't see a foot in front of my face"—got a sick feeling in her stomach. "I panicked," she said.

Her cell phone was back in the car. She reached her husband, and John arrived to help with the search. They repeatedly called the dog's name and then spotted some paw prints leading to a cleared path, a path that was familiar to Augie because John and the dog regularly ran on it.

The path leads into Cambridge's small downtown, and there the Bells were told that the dog had been spotted by a couple running west toward Highway 12/18—also the direction of the Woodhaven subdivision where the Bells live.

They inquired at businesses along the route, and someone said she had seen the dog running west—right in the middle of the highway. "He was running on the highway in front of a truck," Tabatha said. "The truck had slowed down and traffic was backed up behind them. We were told that Augie finally jumped down to the side of the highway and that was the last they saw of him."

Bell recalled: "We were hysterical. He could have been hit by a plow and covered up with snow."

The Search Begins, with Help

They alerted police, they printed posters, they searched on foot. Nothing. It was near dark, and the wind had barely diminished. The Bells trudged home, fearing the worst. On Friday, with still no word, they distributed more posters and continued to search. The temperature had begun to drop.

Friday night, with Augie still missing, Tabatha went to bed, but could barely sleep. What do you do when there is nothing left to do? Bell had heard about people known as "pet communicators." At 3 a.m. Saturday, she turned on her computer.

The woman she found, Karla McKoy, has a business in Washington, Ill.—near Peoria—called Animal Tell. McKoy is a professional animal communicator, which means she claims to communicate telepathically with animals.

"Please keep in mind," McKoy notes on her Web site, "Animal Communication is not an exact science and there is no guarantee that an animal will be found. What I do is from the heart and I receive different information from each animal, so there must be room for broad interpretation."

True Prophecies by Edgar Cayce

Stock Market Crash of 1929—Predicted Seven Months Earlier: There was a division in the money conditions and positions. That fight has hardly begun. When this is an issue we may expect a CONSIDERABLE break and bear market, see? This issue being between those of the reserves of nations and of INDIVIDUALS, and will cause—unless another of the more STABLE banking conditions come to the relief—a great disturbance in financial circles.

World War II—Predicted in 1935: . . . As to the affairs of an international nature, these we find are in a condition of great anxiety on the part of many; not only as individuals but as to nations.

And the activities that have already begun have assumed such proportions that there is to be the attempt upon the part of groups to penalize, or to make for the associations of groups to carry on same.

This will make for the taking of sides, as it were, by various groups or countries or governments. This will be indicated by the Austrians, Germans, and later the Japanese joining in their influence; unseen, and gradually growing to those affairs where there must become, as it were, almost a direct opposition to that which has been the THEME of the Nazis (the Aryan). For these will gradually make for a growing of animosities.

And unless there is interference from what may be called by many the SUPERNATURAL forces and influences, that are activative in the affairs of nations and peoples, the whole WORLD—as it were—will be set on fire by the militaristic groups and those that are "for" power and expansion in such associations. . . .

Edgar Cayce's Association for Research and Enlightenment, Inc.
www.edgarcayce.org.

Her husband, Tabatha said, thought she was crazy. But from the minute she reached McKoy, by phone Saturday morning, there was an instant connection. McKoy sensed things about Augie that only Tabatha knew. She asked: "Is there a problem with his tail?" Bell remembered how Augie had howled when she'd had to lift his tail to clean him a day or so earlier.

"He hated being groomed," she said, hated her lifting his tail.

"The tail's bothering him again," McKoy said. "And he's afraid you're going to groom him." But he was definitely alive. "He's in hibernation mode," she said. "He's afraid to come out."

Bell was encouraged. They continued searching, and she stayed in contact with McKoy. On Sunday—Augie's fourth day missing—the communicator said she was seeing the color blue. Well, Bell thought, there is a sky-blue house in the subdivision. She went over and began searching around the house. The drive had not been shoveled so she figured the people were out of town. She dug around in the snow, and thought sheepishly: "The neighbors are going to call the police on me." She came up empty.

Reunion

Monday, day five, Bell took an even more drastic step. On the Internet she had learned of a man named Harry Oakes, a private investigator in Portland, Ore., who specializes in using his own dog to find missing pets or people. Oakes will, and has, traveled the world in his searches, but one of his best known was right in Portland, and came to light in January when "Dateline NBC" featured him in a child abduction case. Oakes' dog had sniffed out a body but the information was ignored by authorities. Two months later, Oakes was proved right.

Oakes booked a red-eye flight to Chicago. He was to land at 6:45 a.m. Tuesday and connect to Madison an hour later.

It was about the time that Oakes' plane was touching down in Madison that Tabatha Bell's cell phone rang in Cambridge. "Somebody spotted Augie running near the Piggly Wiggly!"

There's a grocery store near the Bells' home.

A few minutes later, another call. "We have your dog in our house." The callers were Sean and Tammy Connery.

Tabatha was ecstatic. She called Oakes with the news, said that she would pay him for his time, and offered to pick him up at the airport. The investigator said that, no, he'd just catch a flight back to Chicago.

The Connery home was a couple of blocks away, and Tabatha knew the house. It was next to the blue house where she'd searched earlier. The Connerys had seen Augie running Tuesday morning, and like everyone in Cambridge, they knew his story. They'd used some treats to get him in the house, and they called the Bells.

When Tabatha got there, Augie was sitting on a couch. He licked her face. Everyone was pretty emotional, including Augie, who was doing fine except for his tail, which was full of burrs.

Periodical Bibliography

The following articles have been selected to supplement the diverse views presented in this chapter.

Chris Colin	"Professionally Adrift? Consult Your Inner Neutrinos," *San Francisco Chronicle*, August 20, 2007.
James Hibberd	"In Search of Today's Ghost Stories: New Technology a Blessing and a Curse for Supernatural Series," *TelevisionWeek*, August 22, 2005.
Olga Kharif	"Scaring Up Paranormal Profits," *BusinessWeek*, May 12, 2005.
Robert E. O'Connor	"Going Out on a Limb to Predict the Future," *Buffalo News*, September 16, 2005.
Lisa Palmer	"Gentle Hands: The Energy Flow in Reiki Promotes Physical, Emotional, and Spiritual Healing," *Better Nutrition*, May 2006.
Danny Penman	"Is this REALLY Proof that Man Can See into the Future? Do Some of Us Avoid Tragedy by Foreseeing It? Some Scientists Now Believe that the Brain Really CAN Predict Events before They Happen," *Daily Mail (London)*, May 5, 2007.
Bill Reed	"Skeptic's Tarot Reading Offers Chance to Reflect on Life, Unknown Future," *Gazette (Colorado Springs, CO)*, January 11, 2005.
Judi Vitale and Alessandra Bogner	"Your 7-Year Feng Shui Forecast," *Marie Claire*, July 2006.
Lizzie Widdicomb	"Skunked: Paranormal Activities in Merchant's House," *New Yorker*, August 27, 2007.
Catherine Zandonella	"Just Passing Through: Welcome to a World Where Teacups Melt through Saucers and Everyone Walks through Walls," *New Scientist*, October 8, 2005.

James Hibberd — "In Search of Today's Ghost Stories: New Technology a Blessing and a Curse for Supernatural Series," *TelevisionWeek*, August 22, 2005.

Olga Kharif — "Scaring Up Paranormal Profits," *BusinessWeek*, May 12, 2005.

Robert E. O'Connor — "Going Out on a Limb to Predict the Future," *Buffalo News*, September 16, 2005.

Lisa Palmer — "Gentle Hands: The Energy Flow in Reiki Promotes Physical, Emotional, and Spiritual Healing," *Better Nutrition*, May 2006.

Danny Penman — "Is this REALLY Proof that Man Can See into the Future? Do Some of Us Avoid Tragedy by Foreseeing It? Some Scientists Now Believe that the Brain Really CAN Predict Events before They Happen," *Daily Mail (London)*, May 5, 2007.

Bill Reed — "Skeptic's Tarot Reading Offers Chance to Reflect on Life, Unknown Future," *Gazette (Colorado Springs, CO)*, January 11, 2005.

Judi Vitale and Alessandra Bogner — "Your 7-Year Feng Shui Forecast," *Marie Claire*, July 2006.

Lizzie Widdicomb — "Skunked: Paranormal Activities in Merchant's House," *New Yorker*, August 27, 2007.

Catherine Zandonella — "Just Passing Through: Welcome to a World Where Teacups Melt through Saucers and Everyone Walks through Walls," *New Scientist*, October 8, 2005.

Are the Mind and Body Separate Entities?

Chapter Preface

A ctor Christopher Reeve became world-famous when he
played Superman in four movies. In 1995, he broke his
neck during a horseback riding accident and became quad-
riplegic. Undaunted by his disability, he spent the remainder
of his life searching for treatments, trying to keep his body
healthy, and acting in and producing movies. He died in October of 2004, the same month that *Reader's Digest* magazine
ran an interview in which he stated, "Your body is not who
you are. The mind and spirit transcend the body."

A 2007 meeting of the World Transhumanist Association
pondered the possibility of someday uploading data from a
human brain to a computer, which would theoretically enable
humans to live forever. In other words, the information in a
human brain could be saved and accessed without a biological
interruption like death. Is that the same as living forever?
Does the mind need a body to be "alive"?

Archaeological discoveries suggest that humans have believed in an afterlife, or at least a preservation of the spirit after death, for tens of thousands of years. In many respects it is
an appealing idea; the thought that people who die do not
permanently disappear is a comforting one. Belief that death
signifies a transition rather than an erasure of an identity can
make grief easier to bear. It can also make death seem less
frightening. Christian notions of Heaven and Hell and Hindu
notions of karma and reincarnation are just two frameworks
that suggest good works (and bad actions) during an Earthly
life do not go unrewarded (or unpunished), which makes suffering and hardship easier to accept. Life after death promises
a second chance to the miserable and eternal bliss to the hon-
orable.

People who believe that the mind or soul merely occupies
the body point to the diversity of cultures promoting such an
idea as evidence that it is true. How else could such different

people develop such similar explanations for what happens when the body is inert? Theories about ghosts, dreams, and spirit travel abound. Skeptics who believe that the mind or soul is attached to the body and can only go where the body goes, however, say that it is natural that so many different people would ponder the same phenomena: sleep, death, and intuition are basic human experiences. Of course diverse cultures will address basic questions in similar ways—all people are human!

As with every controversy, proponents and skeptics of the separation of the mind from the body believe they have amply proven their point. The problem with settling this particular debate is that currently minds can only demonstrate their existence through the medium of a body. Do minds communicate telepathically? Maybe, but we only learn about it after someone uses a mouth or a hand to describe it orally or in writing. Can the spirit leave the body to travel to other places? Maybe, but descriptions of those places could be derived from pictures in books if they are on this planet, and they are unverifiable if they are of planes or dimensions not located in the physical world. Does the soul leave the body at death and live on? Maybe, but no soul has yet confirmed it directly.

In our current mode of existence, minds require bodies to interact with other minds. Even if minds could be uploaded onto a computer in this world, the mind would still require the computer to make its presence known. The necessary link between the mind and a body makes it difficult to design scientific experiments to test the question. Despite evidence from both sides of the argument, no person can know for sure whether or not the mind is separate from the body until/ unless the mind actually leaves the body—and then the mind has no way to report the answer, if it is anywhere at all.

The following chapter explores the relationship of the mind and body and examines the evidence that supports and refutes the possibility that the mind and body are distinct.

> *"People undergoing moderate or severe oxygen starvation may perceive sensations of touch, movement, changes of position, have sensations of floating, or even undergo out-of-body experiences."*

Near-Death Experiences Are Symptoms of a Dying Brain

Dr. G.M. Woerlee

Dr. G.M. Woerlee is an anesthesiologist who has been in practice in the Netherlands for more than twenty-five years. He has long been fascinated with the moment of death, when a person suddenly becomes "absent" and a body becomes a lifeless shell. He has made a career of slowing down and stopping biological functions and is very familiar with how the brain reacts when it is shut down (temporarily or permanently). The following viewpoint details the stages of oxygen deprivation in the brain and compares them to reports about the near-death experiences of dying people.

As you read, consider the following questions:

1. In what ways are people who approach death changed by the experience?

Dr. G.M. Woerlee, *Mortal Minds: The Biology of Near-Death Experiences*. Amherst, NY: Prometheus Books, 2003. Copyright © 2003 by G.M. Woerlee. All rights reserved. Reproduced by permission of De Tijdstroom Publishing Company.

2. How does the author explain the extended religious sojourns into mountains and other places of high elevation?

3. To what does the author attribute the feelings of peace and well-being that often accompany the experience of dying?

Oxygen starvation profoundly affects the functioning of the body, especially the brain and the sense organs. More than nine in ten persons die of disorders where the eternal loss of consciousness of death is ultimately caused by oxygen starvation. This means that the effects of oxygen starvation modify, and determine, the last conscious experiences of more than nine in ten dying people. So to understand the effects of oxygen starvation upon the brain, and the sense organs, is to understand the dying experiences of more than nine in ten people.

There is a vast body of knowledge about the effects of oxygen starvation on the body. Knowledge of these effects of oxygen starvation comes from many sources: from studies of the effects of oxygen starvation upon healthy people, from studies of the effects of oxygen starvation experienced by people during near-death states, and from studies of the effects of oxygen starvation undergone by the dying. All these studies show some organs and tissues are more sensitive to the effects of oxygen starvation than others. Of all the organs and tissues in the body, the brain, and the eyes, are the organs most sensitive to oxygen starvation. . . .

Changes in the functioning of the brain and the eyes caused by increasingly severe oxygen starvation are the same for each person, because each person has the same basic body structure and function, regardless of race, sex, culture, religion, or psyche. . . .

Studies of oxygen starvation show it is possible to divide the effects of oxygen starvation into four distinct degrees:

mild, moderate, severe, and extreme oxygen starvation. A detailed study of the effects of these four degrees of oxygen starvation reveals many aspects of the experience of dying.

Mild and Moderate Oxygen Starvation

Mild oxygen starvation is the mildest degree of oxygen starvation. Mild oxygen starvation does not affect the functioning of the brain or the senses. . . . Moderate oxygen starvation does not cause loss of consciousness, nor does moderate oxygen starvation affect breathing. But moderate oxygen starvation does affect the functioning of the brain and the senses. For example, moderate oxygen starvation always causes malfunction of a part of the brain surface called the 'prefrontal cortex'. The prefrontal cortex is that part of the frontal cortex lying behind the forehead and above the eye cavities. Prefrontal cortex malfunction alters mental processes, causing forgetfulness, causing difficulty concentrating and planning, causing difficulty with mathematical calculations, and always induces an attitude of serene unconcern, of calm and tranquil indifference to everything, including pain. . . .

Feelings of indifference and serenity . . . are typical of prefrontal cortex malfunction. But these changes in mental function caused by oxygen starvation do not immediately return to normal after restoration of normal body function. Indeed, it may take several months, and sometimes even longer than one year before the functioning of the prefrontal cortex returns to normal after a period of severe oxygen starvation. This is why many people notice personality changes after recovering from oxygen starvation severe enough to affect the functioning of their brains. Many people even report becoming calmer, more tolerant, more caring, and even more sociable after a period of oxygen starvation. . . .

Religious Experience

The mental effects of prefrontal cortex malfunction induced by oxygen starvation may even be one of the reasons why holy people seek high, and lonely places to meditate and undergo religious experiences. After climbing high in the mountains, prefrontal cortex malfunction induced by oxygen starvation alters the functioning of their brains. They become unconcerned and indifferent to cold, weariness, and hunger. Wonderful feelings of calm exultation arise, and their mental processes seem unusually keen and sharp. Isolation and fixity of purpose ensure that their feelings of mystical exultation and rapt concentration continue without thought of rest or food for a considerable time. After several weeks, their bodies adapt to the low oxygen pressure in the air they breathe, and their bodies become less oxygen starved. Their feelings of religious exultation fade along with their indifference to hunger and discomfort, and they decide to return to the lowlands. It takes three months to one year before the functioning of the prefrontal cortex returns to normal after several days exposure to moderate oxygen starvation at high altitudes. So these holy people develop long-lasting changes in the functioning of the prefrontal cortex during their sojourn in the mountains. Upon their return to the lowlands, their followers observe the changes caused by their stay in the mountains. They interpret the indifference caused by prefrontal malfunction as a renewed inner calm and transcendence of the world about them. And all are happy, because meditation high in the mountains has indeed wrought wondrous changes. . . .

Letting Go of the Body

Moderate and severe oxygen starvation also induce malfunction of those parts of the brain enabling the conscious mind to perceive sensations of pain, touch, movement, and body position. Malfunction of these regions of the brain, such as the primary somatosensory cortex, the secondary somatosensory cortex, the prefrontal cortex, and the parietal cortex, induce a large variety of sensations in the mind. This is why people undergoing moderate or severe oxygen starvation may perceive sensations of touch, movements, changes of position, have sensations of floating, or even undergo out-of-body experiences. Severe oxygen starvation eventually causes these regions of the brain to cease functioning altogether. So people who are conscious, and in whom the primary somatosensory cortex, the secondary somatosensory cortex, the prefrontal cortex, and the parietal cortex no longer function, are incapable of perceiving sensations of pain, touch, movement, body position, or body image, and may even ignore or forget their bodies altogether. Such blurring, or total loss of the sense of body image and body position, may even result in a disintegration of all sense of space and self, causing affected people to feel a sense of being 'one with the universe'.

Moderate and severe oxygen starvation also induces abnormal nervous activity in a part of the brain called the 'temporal lobe', especially in a part of the temporal lobe called the 'hippocampus', a part of the brain concerned with the formation and recall of memories. Abnormal nervous activity within the structures of the temporal lobes can arouse recall of people and past events, together with the associated sounds, smells, and emotions perceived at that time. Abnormal nervous activity within the structures of the temporal lobes can cause emotions of déjà vu, strange and indescribable emotions, or even emotions such as fear, sadness, or anger. Abnormal nervous activity within the structures of the temporal lobes can induce tingling feelings all over the body, sensations of movement, or feelings of heat or cold. Abnormal nervous activity within the structures of the temporal lobes can arouse visual hallucinations of blinking or flashing lights, of strangers, of friends, and of relatives. Abnormal nervous activity within the structures of the temporal lobes can also arouse auditory hallucinations, such as of music, roaring, clicking, pinging, or buzzing sounds. And abnormal nervous activity within the structures of the temporal lobes can also arouse a powerful

Conversations with God

I have on a number of occasions felt that I had enjoyed a period of intimate communion with the divine. These meetings came unasked and unexpected, and seemed to consist merely in the temporary obliteration of the conventionalities which usually surround and cover my life.... Once it was when from the summit of a high mountain I looked over a gashed and corrugated landscape extending to a long convex of ocean that ascended to the horizon, and again from the same point when I could see nothing beneath me but a boundless expanse of white cloud, on the blown surface of which a few high peaks, including the one I was on, seemed plunging about as if they were dragging their anchors. What I felt on these occasions was a temporary loss of my own identity, accompanied by an illumination which revealed to me a deeper significance than I had been wont to attach to life. It is in this that I find my justification for saying that I have enjoyed communication with God.

William James, The Varieties of Religious Experience, *1908.*

sense of the presence of 'something', or actual hallucinations of entities, of people, or even of gods. . . .

Different Interpretations

People who unexpectedly undergo life-threatening experiences seldom see gods, saints, religious figures, or deceased family members during near-death experiences. This is quite different from near-death experiences undergone by people who expect to die, or know they are dying. These people are more likely to have visions of gods, of saints, of supernatural beings, or of deceased friends and relatives shortly before they die. This difference is difficult to explain by changes in the functioning of the brain. But it is possible that many people believe deep within themselves, that deceased friends and relatives will come to guide them in their passage from the world of the living into the world of the dead. . . .

Comparison of the near-death visions of people living in different countries and societies shows that personal, social, and cultural factors determine the content of these visions. Most differences occur in the religious content of these visions. These differences prove that religious visions are not confirmation of the truth of any particular religion. Instead, these visions prove that personal beliefs, as well as the social and cultural forces moulding each person's life, determine the nature of the religious figures and gods seen during religious visions. A person raised in total ignorance of Christian beliefs, the Christian pantheon, and Christian philosophy, does not have Christian visions, because they know nothing of these things. Their religious visions are of the pantheon and philosophy with which they are familiar, and in which they believe. So a Hindu has Hindu religious visions, a Christian has Christian religious visions, a Buddhist has Buddhist religious visions, a Moslem has Moslem religious visions, and a Zoroastrian has Zoroastrian religious visions. . . .

The reasons for returning to life may differ from one person to another, but one thing is certain, the reasons for returning to life during near-death-experiences are not so much religious, as they are insights into the effects of religion, culture, and individual psychology upon the content of visions aroused by abnormal brain function.

> *"As soon as the function of the brain has been lost, as in clinical death or brain death, memories and consciousness do still exist, but the receptivity is lost, the connection is interrupted."*

Near-Death Experiences Are Symptoms of Consciousness Disconnecting from the Body

Pim van Lommel

Dr. Pim van Lommel is a cardiologist at the Hospital Rijnstate in the Netherlands. He became interested in near-death experiences after years of working with patients who had them during cardiac arrest. The following viewpoint provides information about the brain's structure and function, and claims that consciousness has to be located outside of the body because the brain has a limited capacity to store data. The author suggests an explanation for the continuation of consciousness beyond biological death from the field of quantum physics, and likens the brain to a computer that can connect to the Internet but does not contain the Internet.

Pim van Lommel, "About the Continuity of Our Consciousness," *Brain Death and Disorders of Consciousness (Advances in Experimental Medicine and Biology)*, vol. 550, 2004, pp. 115–132. Copyright © 2004 by Springer Science & Business Media, Inc. Reproduced with kind permission from Springer Science and Business Media and the author.

As you read, consider the following questions:

1. How does quantum physics describe the two aspects of consciousness?

2. In what sense is the human brain like a cellular phone, television set, or laptop computer?

3. In what ways would the discovery of a consciousness separate from the body require western medicine to re-examine its philosophies?

For decades, extensive research has been done to localize consciousness and memories inside the brain, so far without success. In connection with the unproven assumption that consciousness and memories are produced and stored inside the brain, we should ask ourselves how a non-material activity such as concentrated attention or thinking can correspond to an observable (material) reaction in the form of measurable electrical, magnetic, and chemical activity at a certain place in the brain, even an increase in cerebral blood flow is observed during such a non-material activity as thinking. Neurophysiological studies have shown these aforesaid activities through EEG [electroencephalography], magnetoencephalography (MEG), magnetic resonance imaging (MRI) and positron emission tomography (PET) scanning. Specific areas of the brain have been shown to become metabolically active in response to a thought or feeling. However, those studies, although providing evidence for the role of neuronal networks as an intermediary for the manifestation of thoughts, do not necessary imply that those cells also produce the thoughts. . . .

The brain contains about 100 billion neurons, 20 billion of which are situated in the cerebral cortex. Several thousand neurons die each day, and there is a continuous renewal of the proteins and lipids constituting cellular membranes on a time-span basis ranging from several days to a few weeks. During life the cerebral cortex continuously adaptively modifies its neuronal network, including changing the number and location of synapses. All neurons show an electrical potential across their cell membranes, and each neuron has tens to hundreds of synapses that influence other neurons. Transportation of information along neurons occurs predominantly by means of action potentials, differences in membrane potential caused by synaptic depolarization and hyperpolarization. The sum total of changes along neurons causes transient electric fields and therefore also transient magnetic fields along the synchronously activated dendrites. . . .

Some researchers try to create artificial intelligence by computer technology, hoping to simulate programs evoking consciousness. But Roger Penrose, a quantum physicist, argues that "Algorithmic computations cannot simulate mathematical reasoning. The brain, as a closed system capable of internal and consistent computations, is insufficient to elicit human consciousness." Penrose offers a quantum mechanical hypothesis to explain the relation between consciousness and the brain. And Simon Berkovitch, a professor in Computer Science of the George Washington University, has calculated that the brain has an absolutely inadequate capacity to produce and store all the informational processes of all our memories with associative thoughts. We would need 10^{24} operations per second, which is absolutely impossible for our neurons. Herms Romijn, a Dutch neurobiologist, comes to the same conclusion. One should conclude that the brain has not enough computing capacity to store all the memories with associative thoughts from one's life, has not enough retrieval abilities, and seems not to be able to elicit consciousness.

Consciousness Is in "Phase-Space"

With our current medical and scientific concepts it seems impossible to explain all aspects of the subjective experiences as reported by patients with an NDE [near-death experience] during their period of cardiac arrest, during a transient loss of all functions of the brain. But science, I believe, is the search for explaining new mysteries rather than the cataloguing of old facts and concepts. So it is a scientific challenge to discuss new hypotheses that could explain the reported *interconnectedness* with the consciousness of other persons and of deceased relatives, to explain the possibility to experience instantaneously and simultaneously (*non-locality*) a review and a preview of someone's life in a *dimension without our conventional body-linked concept of time and space,* where all past, present and future events exist, and the possibility to have clear consciousness with memories from early childhood, with self-identity, with cognition, and with emotion, and the possibility of perception out and above one's lifeless body.

We should conclude, like many others, that quantum mechanical processes could have something critical to do with how consciousness and memories relate with the brain and the body during normal daily activities as well as during brain death or clinical death. . . .

Phase-space is an invisible, non-local, higher-dimensional space consisting of *fields of probability,* where every past and future event is available as a possibility. Within this phase-space no matter is present, everything belongs to uncertainty, and neither measurements nor observations are possible by physicists. . . .

The Body Is in Real-Space

Quantum physics cannot explain the essence of consciousness or the secret of life, but in my concept it is helpful for understanding the transition between the fields of consciousness in the phase-space (to be compared with the probability fields as we know from quantum mechanics) and the body-linked waking consciousness in the real-space, because these are the two *complementary* aspects of consciousness. Our whole and undivided consciousness with declarative memories finds its origin in, and is stored in this phase-space, and the cortex only serves as a relay station for parts of our consciousness and parts of our memories to be received into our waking consciousness. In this concept consciousness is not physically rooted. This could be compared with the Internet, which does not originate from the computer itself, but is only received by it.

Life creates the transition from phase-space into our manifest real-space; according to our hypothesis life creates the possibility to receive the fields of consciousness (waves) into the waking consciousness which belongs to our physical body (particles). During life, our consciousness has an aspect of waves as well as of particles, and there is a permanent interaction between these two aspects of consciousness. . . . The particle aspect, the physical aspect of consciousness in the material world, originates from the wave aspect of our consciousness from the phase-space by collapse of the wave function into particles ("objective reduction"), and can be measured by means of EEG, MEG, MRI, and PET scan. And different neuronal networks function as interface for different aspects of our consciousness, as can be demonstrated by changing images during these registrations of EEG, MRI or PET scan. The wave aspect of our indestructible consciousness in phase-space, with non-local interconnectedness, is inherently not measurable by physical means. When we die, our consciousness will no longer have an aspect of particles, but only an eternal aspect of waves.

With this new concept about consciousness and the mind-brain relation all reported elements of an NDE during cardiac arrest could be explained. This concept is also compatible with the non-local interconnectedness with fields of consciousness of other persons in phase-space. Following an NDE most people, often to their own amazement and confusion, experience an enhanced intuitive sensibility, like clairvoyance and clairaudience, or prognostic dreams, in which they "dream" about future events. In people with an NDE the functional receiving capacity seems to be permanently enhanced. When you compare this with a TV set, you receive not only

Hypothesis Concerning Soul Substance (1907)

The soul substance so necessary to the conception of continuing personal identity, after the death of this material body, must still be a form of gravitative matter, or perhaps a middle form of substance neither gravitative matter or ether, not capable of being weighed, and yet not identical with ether. Since however the substance considered in our hypothesis is linked organically with the body until death takes place, it appears to me more reasonable to think that it must be some form of gravitative matter, and therefore capable of being detected at death by weighing a human being in the act of death.

My first subject was a man dying of tuberculosis. . .

The patient was under observation for three hours and forty minutes before death, lying on a bed arranged on a light framework built upon very delicately balanced platform beam scales.

The patient's comfort was looked after in every way, although he was practically moribund when placed upon the bed. He lost weight slowly at the rate of one ounce per hour due to evaporation of moisture in respiration and evaporation of sweat.

During all three hours and forty minutes I kept the beam end slightly above balance near the upper limiting bar in order to make the test more decisive if it should come.

At the end of three hours and forty minutes he expired and suddenly coincident with death the beam end dropped with an audible stroke hitting against the lower limiting bar and remaining there with no rebound. The loss was ascertained to be three-fourths of an ounce.

Duncan MacDougall, "Hypothesis Concerning Soul Substance Together with Experimental Evidence of the Existence of Such Substance," American Medicine, *April, 2007.*

Channel 1, the transmission of your personal consciousness, but simultaneously Channels 2, 3 and 4 with aspects of consciousness of others. . . .

Consciousness Is Like Television

In trying to understand this concept of quantum mechanical mutual interaction between the invisible phase-space and our visible, material body, it seems appropriate to compare it with modern worldwide communication. There is a continuous exchange of objective information by means of electromagnetic fields for radio, TV, mobile telephone, or laptop computer. We are unaware of the vast amounts of electromagnetic fields that constantly, day and night, exist around us and through us, as well as through structures like walls and buildings. We only become aware of these electromagnetic informational fields at the moment we use our mobile telephone or by switching on our radio, TV or laptop. What we receive is not inside the instrument, nor in the components, but thanks to the receiver, the information from the electromagnetic fields becomes observable to our senses and hence perception occurs in our consciousness. The voice we hear over our telephone is not inside the telephone. The concert we hear over our radio is transmitted to our radio. The images and music we hear and see on TV are transmitted to our TV set. The Internet is not located inside our laptop. We can receive what is transmitted with the speed of light from a distance of some hundreds or thousands of miles. And if we switch off the TV set, the reception disappears, but the transmission continues. The information transmitted remains present within the electromagnetic fields. The connection has been interrupted, but it has not vanished and can still be received elsewhere by using another TV set (*"non-locality"*).

Could our brain be compared to the TV set, which receives electromagnetic waves and transforms them into image and sound, as well as to the TV camera, which transforms image and sound into electromagnetic waves? This electromagnetic radiation holds the essence of all information, but is only perceivable by our senses through suitable instruments like cameras and TV sets.

The informational fields of our consciousness and of our memories, both evolving during our lifetime by our experiences and by the informational input from our sense organs, are present around us and become available to our waking consciousness only through our functioning brain (and other cells of our body) in the shape of electromagnetic fields. As soon as the function of the brain has been lost, as in clinical death or brain death, memories and consciousness do still exist, but the receptivity is lost, the connection is interrupted.

Turning the TV Off

According to our concept, grounded on the reported aspects of consciousness experienced during cardiac arrest, we can conclude that our consciousness could be based on fields of information, consisting of waves, and that it originates in the phase-space. During cardiac arrest, the functioning of the brain and of other cells in our body stops because of anoxia. The electromagnetic fields of our neurons and other cells disappear, and the possibility of resonance, the interface between consciousness and physical body, is interrupted. . . .

The conclusion that consciousness can be experienced independently of brain function might well induce a huge change in the scientific paradigm in western medicine, and could have practical implications in actual medical and ethical problems such as the care for comatose or dying patients, euthanasia, abortion, and the removal of organs for transplantation from somebody in the dying process with a beating heart in a warm body but a diagnosis of brain death.

There are still more questions than answers, but, based on the aforementioned theoretical aspects of the obviously experienced continuity of our consciousness, we finally should consider the possibility that death, like birth, may well be a mere passing from one state of consciousness to another.

> "*Mediums claim that the stimuli are there for all to perceive, but they're low-level and subtle, and most of us are too distracted by the outside world as well as our own thoughts and feelings to sense them.*"

Mediums Communicate with the Dead

Gary E. Schwartz and William L. Simon

Dr. Gary E. Schwartz is a professor of psychology, neurology, and psychiatry at the University of Arizona, and director of its Human Energy Systems Laboratory. William L. Simon is a published author, and screen and television writer. The following viewpoint is an excerpt from The Afterlife Experiments, *a collaborative exploration of current research being conducted with spiritual mediums who communicate with the souls/spirits/consciousness of people who have died. Such experiments are highly controversial, and the validity of their results is often questioned.*

As you read, consider the following questions:

1. Is the explanation about why mediums are unable to perform for nonbelievers a satisfactory answer to the skeptics' question?

2. How are mediums able to pass along messages from dead people who speak foreign languages?

3. Why do mediums pass along only messages of love instead of information that could help mankind?

A Question Posed by Skeptics

Can mediums read skeptics? If mediums can read only believers, this raises serious questions about the claims.

One way of responding to this valid challenge is to turn to psychological studies on what's called "the perception of weak stimuli," which deals with how people respond to very faint inputs.

Experimental psychologists have conducted research with very soft sounds—so low that it takes careful attention to detect them. If a loud sound is played just before the soft sound, the listener will miss the following gentle sound. The previous loud sound serves as a distracting stimulus.

Distraction operates for strong stimuli as well. Basketball players tell us that it's harder to make foul shots when opposing fans are screaming for them to miss.

In the same way, mediums tell us that in order to receive information, which is typically soft and subtle, they must get their own thoughts and emotions out of the way. Their own feelings deafen them, so to speak, to the subtle information they're trying to receive.

Our dream team of mediums tells us that when they face hostile clients or a hostile audience, they get anxious. They have negative thoughts and feelings that distract them from getting the subtle information they're trying to receive. Some say they're reminded of being teased when they were children;

they worry about missing the shot and then being laughed at, or worse. And they know the skeptics will claim "See, you can't do it—it must be fraud."

Of course, if the mediums were engaged in fraud, it shouldn't matter whether they were reading believers or skeptics. If they had detectives secretly getting information ahead of time, for example, the facts obtained in advance would be there for the mediums to use no matter how skeptical the sitter.

On the face of it, at least, the mediums' explanation of why they don't like to read for skeptics appears reasonable. Maybe it really is more difficult—for well-established cognitive information-processing reasons. But this will be a valuable question to be addressed in future research.

A Second Question

If mediums can really hear dead people, why don't they ever hear and speak in foreign languages or make medical diagnoses from a dead physician? If mediums can hear only what they know, maybe they're just replaying their own memories and fantasies.

Mediums claim that the stimuli are there for all to perceive, but they're low-level and subtle, and most of us are too distracted by the outside world as well as our own thoughts and feelings to sense them.

Much of what we hear is incomplete, but we're usually able to fill in the gaps. For example, if you're watching a romantic movie on television in a noisy room and you pick up an incomplete group of sounds—"I ov er"—you would very likely be able to fill in what's missing and, without even realizing you didn't get all the sounds, understand that what the character really said was "I love her." This kind of "fill-in" phenomenon has been substantially investigated in contemporary cognitive psychology.

Now, instead, imagine that the character in the film has said a group of sounds which, over the noise in the room, reached you as "J a or." You wonder, "What did he say? I missed it." But if you knew French, your mind might have been able to fill in the gaps to complete the sentence—"Je l'adore"—which means the same thing as before: "I love her." (Well, okay, it could also mean "I love him" or "I love it." Leave it to the French to be nonspecific, even about love.)

Experimental psychology tells us that we often unconsciously fill in subtle or incomplete information with the information we know—the information from our own memories. That is, at least, a reasonable-sounding explanation of why mediums shouldn't be expected to relay messages in languages they don't understand, on highly technical jargon or medical terminology unfamiliar to them. Again, a subject for future experimentation.

In this regard, our team of mediums tell us that symbols from their own personal lives often come to them, and they learn how to interpret these symbols. I've found [television psychic and medium] John Edward especially surprising and often amusing in this regard. As we've seen, his video-store job as a youngster sometimes leads him to get the names of images from movies that have a connection with something a deceased is trying to communicate. . . .

Another Question

Why do dead people always give such boring information like messages of love and the like? Why don't they give us information about new science or technology? It sounds as though the mediums are just giving the clients what they want to hear. . . .

This is a troubling question. Perhaps the answer might lie along the following line of reasoning: Imagine a deceased person, a father who has been waiting for months or even years to communicate with his daughter. His time with the high-priced medium is maybe five minutes or, if he's lucky,

So You Want to Visit a Medium

Not everyone who calls a medium for an appointment really understands what a medium does or what to expect in a reading. Sometimes people call mediums for the right reasons, and sometimes they call mediums when they should be calling for another kind of help. As your coach, my first step will be to make sure you understand the best reasons to see a medium.

Sometimes I get calls from people looking for a reading when what they really need to do is call a doctor to check their health, or a career counselor to explore various avenues of work, or a therapist to work out their emotional problems. I am not a doctor, career counselor, or therapist, and it would not be right for me to try to help people with such problems. I also get calls from people who need an astrologer, a card reader, or a psychic rather than a medium.

Carol Lynne, How to Get a Good Reading from a Psychic Medium: Get the Most out of Your Contact with the Other Side, *2003.*

perhaps as much as fifteen. There are other deceased people who want to communicate, too.

What will he want to tell his daughter? The latest scientific discoveries? The great books he's been reading in the afterlife? That's not what his daughter came to hear. And she probably wouldn't believe any of it even if true.

He and his daughter are with the medium for one reason—to give and receive expressions of love. He is there first and foremost to somehow prove to his daughter, in a way she can understand, that he still exists. Not only that, but he wants to prove to her that he still cares—that he is still her father, and that if he has anything to say about it, he will be her father forever.

So he attempts to show the medium who he is, identifying himself by relating information the daughter would know. He then shows his daughter that he's still around by acknowledging present things in her life that she can verify to be true. And he tells her, in his personal way, that he loves her. This is what he wants to do during the little time he has with the medium. . . .

However, [the question] is a thoughtful, provocative one. What would happen if we took the suggestion seriously? What would happen if we took a group of great mediums and invited them to communicate with departed great scientists like Sir James Clerk Maxwell and Professor William James? What would happen if we honored the possibility of the living soul hypothesis and asked them for their help?

Is it possible that we will one day be able to get information in this way, to help sick people whom modern science has no answers for, to solve perplexing problems in the sciences and technology, perhaps to offer suggestions toward furthering world peace? True visionaries are people who conceive of things that most people consider impossible. . . .

Understanding Skepticism

When mediums themselves have trouble believing that what they're doing could be real and come to the conclusion that "It's never enough," how can we expect well-conditioned agnostics and professional skeptics ever to conclude, "I've seen enough to change my mind?". . .

Research suggests there are deep psychological reasons why many of us, not just professional skeptics, have a hard time believing.

Recall the familiar experiments a hundred years ago by Russian physiologist Ivan Pavlov, who conditioned dogs to salivate whenever they heard a bell. I've come to realize that many people in contemporary society, including myself, suffer from an insidious form of conditioned neurosis. We've been conditioned since childhood to pair words like *soul, spirit,* and *survival of consciousness* with negative terms like *stupid, impossible, fake, crazy, shameful, sinful, superstitious, mistaken,* and even *"too good to be true."* Our beliefs are so thoroughly conditioned that even in the face of controlled laboratory experiments, strong negative emotions are triggered by the findings. We think "impossible" or "fraud" or "it's too good to be true" automatically and uncontrollably. . . .

Thoughtful skeptics who are serious scientists are beginning to ask the same question. Professor Ray Hyman, one of the most distinguished academic skeptics, has told me, "I do not have control over my beliefs." He had learned from childhood that paranormal events are impossible. Today he finds himself amazed that even in the face of compelling theory and convincing scientific data, his beliefs have not changed. His repeated disappointments with past genuine frauds prevent him from accepting genuine science today.

Perhaps professional skeptics share a hazard with professional civil engineers: if a civil engineer designs a single bridge that falls down, he almost certainly loses his reputation and his livelihood. If science reveals that one of a skeptic's biggest conceptual bridges has fallen down—for example, the conviction that all mediums are "pretending"—the skeptic could lose his reputation and his livelihood. And once that bridge has fallen, who knows what else may fall?

> *"Once the observer or client has been struck with the apparent accuracy of the reading, it becomes virtually impossible to dislodge the belief in the uniqueness and specificity of the reading."*

Mediums Do Not Communicate with the Dead

Ray Hyman

Dr. Ray Hyman is professor emeritus of psychology at the University of Oregon, Eugene. He is an outspoken critic of parapsychology. The following viewpoint appeared in the magazine Skeptical Inquirer, *and disputes the claims made by Dr. Gary Schwartz regarding his book,* The Afterlife Experiments, *an investigation of the ability of mediums to communicate with the dead. Hyman argues that mediums give vague readings that could apply to any sitter (client), but that sitters are predisposed to believe the mediums, and so interpret ambiguous information as uniquely pertaining to their lives; the successes demonstrate nothing more than rater bias.*

As you read, consider the following questions:

1. Why does the author say that mediums appear successful because of the "illusion of specificity"?

2. How does rater bias on the part of the sitter affect the apparent accuracy of the psychic reading about "Big HN"?

3. What factors suggest that the sitter GD wants the medium's reading to be true?

[D r. Gary] Schwartz has reported a number of studies in which he and his coworkers have observed some talented mediums such as John Edward and George Anderson give readings to sitters in his laboratory. This work has attracted considerable attention because of Schwartz's credentials and position [he formerly taught at Harvard and Yale]. Even more eye-opening is Schwartz's apparent endorsement of the mediums' claims that they are actually communicating with the dead. . . .

He insists that the mediums, although often wrong, consistently came up with specific facts and names about the sitters' departed friends and relatives that the skeptics have been unable to explain away as fraud, cold reading, or lucky guesses. He provides several examples of such instances throughout the book. These examples demonstrate, he believes, that the readings given by his mediums are clearly different from those given by cold readers and less gifted psychics. "If cold readings are easy to spot by anyone familiar with the techniques, the kinds of readings we have been getting," he asserts, "in our laboratory are quite different in character." . . .

Psychologists have uncovered a number of factors that can make an ambiguous reading seem highly specific, unique, and uncannily accurate. And once the observer or client has been struck with the apparent accuracy of the reading, it becomes virtually impossible to dislodge the belief in the uniqueness and specificity of the reading. Research from many areas demonstrates this finding. The principles go under such names as the fallacy of personal validation, subjective validation, confirmation bias, belief perseverance, the illusion of invulnerability, compliance, demand characteristics, false uniqueness effect, foot-in-the-door phenomenon, illusory correlation, integrative agreements, self-reference effect, the principle of individuation, and many, many others. Much of this is facilitated by the illusion of specificity that surrounds language. All language is inherently ambiguous and depends much more than we realize upon the context and nonlinguistic cues to fix its meaning in a given situation. . . .

Accuracy Is Subjective

The very first example of a reading provided in this book begins as follows:

> The first thing being shown to me is a male figure that I would say as being above, that would be to me some type of father image. . . . Showing me the month of May. . . . They're telling me to talk about the Big H—um, the H connection. To me this an H with an N sound. So what they are talking about is Henna. Henry, but there's an HN connection. (p. xix)

The sitter identified this description as applying to her late husband, Henry. His name was Henry, he died in the month of May and was "affectionately referred to as the 'gentle giant.'" The sitter was able to identify other statements by the medium as applying to her deceased spouse.

Note, however, the huge degree of latitude for the sitter to fit such statements to her personal situation. The phrase "some type of father image" can refer to her husband because he was also the father to her children. However, it could also refer to her own father, her grandfather, someone else's father, or any male with children. It could easily refer to someone without children such as a priest or father-like individual—including

CRYSTAL BALLS

"We have three new models to choose from: Scam, Swindle and Extort."

Cartoon by Mike Baldwin. CartoonStock.com.

Santa Claus. It would have been just as good a match if her husband had been born in May, had married in May, had been diagnosed with a life-threatening illness in May, or considered May as his favorite month. The "HN" connection would fit just as well if the sitter's name were Henna or her husband had a dog named Hank.

Schwartz concludes that, "No other person in the sitter's family fit the cluster of facts 'father image, Big H, Henry, month of May' except her late husband, Henry." Of course not! If that person, or any other, also found a match for their personal life, it too would be unique. When I put myself in the shoes of a possible sitter and try to fit the reading to my situation. I can find a good fit to my father, who was physically large, whose last name was Hyman, and for whom, like any human on this planet, experienced one or more notable events in the month of May. Other things in the reading also can easily be fitted to my father. Neither the original sitter nor anyone else would fit this cluster of facts! Schwartz makes much of the fact that the cluster of facts that a sitter extracts from a reading tend to be unique for that sitter. He even calculates the conditional probabilities of such a cluster occurring just by chance. Naturally, these conditional probabilities are extremely low—often with odds of over a trillion-to-one against chance.

The "accuracy" score for the medium, as calculated by the experimenters, depends critically on the sitter's ratings. This allows subjective validation and uncontrolled rater biases to enter the picture on the side of the mediums. The sitters were deliberately selected because they were already disposed towards the survival hypothesis (that consciousness survives death). Given the statement "some type of father image," the sitter easily fit this to her late husband who was the father of her children. For her, this would get the highest accuracy rating. A more skeptical sitter, realizing the ambiguity in the statement, might give it a lower rating. Given the statement, "showing me the month of May," the committed sitter would rate it accurate because her husband actually died in the month of May. A less committed sitter might rate it as less accurate because she realizes that this statement could apply to any significant event that happened to her husband, herself, or her family in May. From the example above, if I were a committed sitter receiving the same reading, I could see myself giving it a score of five out of five (or 100% accuracy) because my father (obviously a type of father image), experienced one or more significant events in May (*showing me the month of*

May), was large and overweight and named Hyman (*about the Big H—um, the H connection. . .an H with an N sound*). . . .

A "Blind" Experiment: Two Readings

Comparing the two readings that [the medium Laurie] Campbell gave GD [the sitter], I find little to support the claim that the second one replicates the apparent success of the first one. Although a full transcript of the first GD reading is still not available [as of February, 2003], what was included in the first report strongly suggests that the second reading cannot be considered to be aimed at the same individual for whom the first one was given. GD's major interest in mediumship is to establish contact with his deceased partner Michael. Campbell is given credit in the first reading for stating that there was a deceased friend named Michael and then later that he was the primary person for this sitter. The name Michael or a deceased partner does not come up in the second reading. Ironically, the name Michael does appear in the control reading. In the first reading Laurie Campbell mentions a strange name that sounded like *Talya, Tiya,* or *Tilya.* GD stated that he indeed had a friend (living) named Tallia. No such name appears in the second reading. Indeed, of the twenty names Campbell produced in the first reading only three come up in the second reading, and these are such common ones as *George, Robert* or *Bob,* and *Joe* or *Joseph.* In none of these three cases does she identify whether the person is living or dead or what relationship he has to GD. None of the "specific" facts that she apparently stated during the first reading come up in the second one.

Schwartz claims that the rater bias could not have affected the ratings of this double-blind experiment. A look at GD's dazzle shots [accurate statements] and his discussion of the hit and miss data suggests otherwise. His first dazzle shot is "Bob or Robert [the name of his father]." These names occur early in the reading in a statement that goes. "And then I could feel like what I thought was like a divine presence and the feeling of a name Mary or Bob or Robert." This appears in a context with other names and other general statements, none of which even hint of a father. The second dazzle shot is "George [GD's first name]." Again this appears in a context with no hint that this could be referring to the sitter. Campbell states, "I got like some names like a Lynn, or Kristie, a George." His third dazzle shot is the statement, "I had the feeling of a presence of an Aunt." GD identifies this aunt as his aunt Alice, although Campbell does not provide the name Alice anywhere in the reading. I count at least twenty-seven names thrown out by Campbell during this second reading. Actually, she covers a much broader range of names because she typically casts a wide net with statements like: "And an 'M' name. More like a Margaret, or Martha, or Marie, something with an 'M.'" It is up to the sitter to find a match. As indicated by his dazzle shots, GD is strongly disposed to do so. . . .

Instead of assuming that Campbell was somehow conveying information to GD from his departed relatives, it is just as plausible to assume that once GD decided that the actual transcript was meant for him, then subjective validation took over and did the rest. . . . From then on, he would read that transcript as if it were truly describing his departed relatives and reject the other as not relevant.

This conjecture fits well with everything we know about subjective validation and the acceptance of personality sketches that one believes was meant for one's self. Is this farfetched in GD's case? To me, it seems quite obvious just reading the transcript and looking at GD's ratings. The entire case for the reading's validity is based on the assumption that Campbell is describing GD's summer vacation home on Lake Erie in upstate New York. Given this assumption everything is then interpreted within this context. Of course, Campbell never states that she is describing a summer vacation home. It is GD who makes this connection. As just one of many examples of how

GD is creative in making the reading fit his circumstances, he gives Campbell credit for having identified the color of their summer cottage which was painted yellow with white trim on the windows. Campbell does, at one point, say, "And I kept getting colors of like yellow and white." This is in a context where she is talking about a woman who spends all her time in the kitchen. One could construe this as perhaps describing the interior colors of the kitchen, the woman's clothing, the old mixer she is described as using, among other possibilities. However, the statement is far removed for any mention of the exterior of the house as such. Earlier in the reading she mentions a white house. A little bit further on, she again mentions a house. She immediately follows this with "And I kept seeing the colors of like grays and blues, but that looked real weathered." Obviously, if the house had been gray and blue, Campbell would have been given credit for a direct hit. GD manages to ignore this and gives Campbell credit for having correctly described the house as yellow and white.

Again, I suspect that Schwartz will disagree with my interpretation. After all, he has already gone on record that this study "provided incontrovertible evidence in response to the skeptics' highly implausible argument against the single-blind study that the sitter would be biased in his or her ratings (for example, misrating his deceased loved ones' names and relationships) because he knew that this information was from his own reading." Nevertheless, the data are quite consistent with the possibility that all we have to do to account for his "breathtaking" findings is to assume that they are due to rater bias.

> *"Six weeks after breaking their ankles, patients being treated with hypnotherapy were three weeks ahead in their healing schedule than those who were just put in plaster."*

Belief Is Sufficient to Cure Illness

Roger Dobson

Roger Dobson is a reporter for the United Kingdom newspaper, The Independent. In the following viewpoint, he describes many ways that hypnotism is being used in medical care to treat minor ailments and major health concerns. Hypnotism is viewed with suspicion by many people, but the media have traditionally focused on cinematic portrayals of hypnotism as a method of control. People who are taught to use hypnotism, however, use it for their own benefit and manage their health from modifying snoring behavior to reducing dental pain and even alleviating some of the symptoms of cystic fibrosis.

As you read, consider the following questions:

1. Why is hypnotism generally looked upon with suspicion?

2. How has hypnotherapy helped people with heart trouble?

3. How does a therapist help a patient achieve a hypnotic state?

There's no magic, no swinging pendulums or swaying watches, and no one is counting backwards as they slump into unconsciousness. This is medical rather than stage or movie hypnotism, and it is increasingly being used to treat the symptoms of diseases and conditions as diverse as asthma, cystic fibrosis, snoring, migraines and warts.

It's been used to allow surgery and dental work without anaesthesia, and for pain-free childbirth without medication. And new evidence from the UK's first and only NHS [National Health Service] centre offering hypnotherapy shows that it's highly effective in treating some types of chest pain as well as irritable bowel syndrome.

New research from America has also found that more than half the people who used hypnotherapy to give up smoking were able to kick the habit, while researchers in France have successfully used the therapy to lower blood pressure.

Hypnosis Regains Popularity

Hypnosis has been used for centuries to treat diverse ills, but it went into relative decline with the rise of modern medicine, and in the last 200 years it's been more associated with stage magicians and movie villains than medicine.

Film-makers take a lot of blame for damaging the image of hypnotism: "When a hypnotist appears on screen, expect evil. If his induction features magnetic hand passes, he's probably about to compel someone to commit a crime. If he hypnotises with an intense stare, his intent is likelier seduction," says Dr Deirdre Barrett of Harvard Medical School, who has studied more than 200 films about hypnotism.

At the University Hospital of South Manchester, Professor Peter Whorwell, a gastroenterologist who heads the only NHS

[National Health Service]-funded hypnotherapy centre in Britain, which has been pioneering the therapy as a treatment of irritable bowel syndrome [IBS], agrees. "One of the problems is the name," he says. "If we started off again with a name like neuromodulation, for example, it would be more readily accepted. The name hypnotism has so much baggage attached. Cognitive behavioural therapy is now reasonably well accepted, and so, too, is psychotherapy, but of the three, I would say hypnotism is potentially the most powerful. It is becoming a treatment of choice for IBS.

"When I am dead and gone, people are going to suddenly realise that hypnotism is an incredibly powerful tool and question why it has been ignored for so long."

Completely Focused Attention

Just how it works is not clear, and some critics suggest it's simply a way of relaxing. But practitioners say there's more to it, and that under hypnosis the patient can concentrate intensely on a specific thought, memory, feeling or sensation while blocking out distractions.

"The first thing you have to do is get past the myths and misconceptions about clinical hypnosis," says Dr Carol Ginandes who led a study into its use for anxiety at Harvard Medical School. "It's not used for entertainment. There are no Svengali-like figures [in power-] dominant relationships. It's not a sleep state or something that someone can make you do. It's a state of heightened, focused attention that we can all shift into very naturally."

In a report in the Harvard Magazine, she explains how it has an effect: "We don't yet understand the mechanisms by which these suggestions are transplanted by the mind into the language of the body, but let's say someone is a smoker. When he's in a hypnotic state, I could suggest that he's going to find himself craving cigarettes less and less over a period of time. If he's ready to quit, that suggestion will be planted at a deep level in his mind, like seeds planted beneath the soil rather than scattered over the top, helping him tap into some useful physical and psychological resources."

Cures Many Ills

Smoking

In a study at the Scott and White Memorial Hospital in Texas, smokers were given eight sessions of therapy over two months, and told to quit smoking one week after beginning the course of treatment.

Carbon-monoxide concentration tests were carried out on the patients to see whether they had smoked after treatment, and results showed that by the end of treatment 40 per cent had given up. At a follow-up 12 weeks later, 60 per cent had quit.

Dental

Hypnotherapy is increasingly being used in a number of areas of dentistry, including dental phobia, teeth-grinding and extractions and fillings. It has also been used for dental surgery that is usually done under local or general anaesthetic.

In one reported case, a patient in Scotland has also had a tooth implant, which involved putting a titanium rod into her jaw. In her case, hypnosis was used to alter the sensation in the areas where surgery was taking place. She was asked to imagine a dial where zero meant no pain.

Chest Pains

Up to one-third of patients who have angina-like chest pain are found to have normal coronary arteries, but many continue to suffer painful symptoms despite no evidence of heart disease. Non-cardiac chest pain is a problem because there is little or no treatment.

In a new NHS-funded trial at Manchester, 28 patients were given 12 sessions of hypnotherapy or a placebo treatment. After being hypnotised, patients were told to focus on the chest, and given repetitive suggestions about reducing

In-Vitro Fertilization (IVF) and Embryo Transplantation (ET) Outcomes

Experimental Group: 98 treatment cycles under hypnosis (with 89 women)
Control Group: 96 treatment cycles without hypnosis (with 96 women)

	Hypnosis ET	Regular ET
Number of clinical pregnancies	52	29
Pregnancy Rate per Patient	58.4%	30.2%
Pregnancy Rate per Cycle	53.1%	30.2%
Implementation Rate	28%	14.4%

TAKEN FROM: E. Levitas et al. "Hypnosis and IVF Outcome," *Fertility and Sterility*, 2006.

pain. Patients were also given a tape of a session and encouraged to practise at home. Results show that of those who had the therapy, eight out of 10 had an all-round improvement in symptoms.

Wound Healing

Researchers at Harvard Medical School have shown that broken bones and surgical wounds heal faster in patients who have hypnotherapy. Six weeks after breaking their ankles, patients being treated with hypnotherapy were three weeks ahead in their healing schedule than those who were just put in plaster.

In a second study, the researchers had similar results with surgical wounds. Before surgery, suggestions were made under therapy on pain and anxiety, and on decreased inflammation, reduced scar tissue, and accelerated wound-healing. Results show the women who had the therapy healed significantly faster.

Irritable Bowel Syndrome

One of the most common gastrointestinal disorders, with research showing that between five and 20 per cent of us suffer at some time. Its main symptoms include abdominal pain, diarrhoea or constipation. The exact cause is not known, but in some people changes in the balance of bacteria that line the gut are thought to be involved, as well as inflammation. Existing treatment for the condition can be only moderately effective.

Research at the University Hospital of South Manchester, where the first trial of hypnotherapy for the condition was carried out, shows that the majority of sufferers can benefit. "We have found that IBS patients treated with hypnotherapy remain well in the long term, with dramatically reduced medication needs," say the researchers.

Cystic Fibrosis

According to a University of Michigan report, hypnotherapy can reduce symptoms of cough, shortness of breath, anxiety and other symptoms of cystic fibrosis.

A study at the Robert C. Schwartz Cystic Fibrosis Center at the State University of New York also shows that self-hypnosis can be highly effective. "Many of the patients used hypnosis for more than one purpose, including relaxation (61 per cent of patients), relief of pain associated with medical procedures (31 per cent), headache relief (16 per cent), changing the taste of medications to make the flavour more palatable (10 per cent), and control of other symptoms associated with CF (18 per cent). The patients successfully utilised self-hypnosis 86 per cent of the time."

Childbirth

Research at the Women's and Children's Hospital in Adelaide, where hypnosis is used for women in labour, shows it is highly effective. Women who has the therapy, which was given after 37 weeks gestation, used fewer epidurals—36 per cent compared with 53 per cent in other women. A second study showed that women taught self-hypnosis reduced their need for analgesia by half, epidurals by 70 per cent, and were more than twice as likely to be satisfied with their pain management in labour compared with other women.

Snoring

According to Harley Street psychiatrist Dr Tom Kraft, snoring can be treated with hypnotherapy by suggesting under hypnosis that the sufferer turns on his side every time he begins to snore.

"I have reported on the case of a 53-year-old man who came to see me after his snoring led to his wife throwing him out of the bedroom," he says. "After I treated him, his snoring went, and he was allowed back in the bedroom, for which he was eternally grateful. After 10 sessions, the patient no longer snored, and when he was followed up later the improvements had been maintained."

A Sense of Security

What hypnotism doesn't do is put people to sleep, or make them lose control, or do things against their will. "Many see it as the mind being taken over by the hypnotist and loss of control, which is completely erroneous," says Professor Peter Whorwell at the University Hospital of South Manchester. "As a consequence of this, the whole subject is surrounded by a cloud of mystery."

In hypnotherapy, patients are helped by the therapist to reach what's described as a relaxed state of consciousness, like being absorbed in a good book. Therapists may start by describing images that create a sense of security and well-being. They may then suggest ways of achieving specific goals, such as getting rid of phobias.

Just how it works is not clear. Practitioners say the patient can concentrate intensely on a specific thought, memory, feeling or sensation while blocking out distractions.

> *"Belief and expectation, cardinal components of hope, can block pain by releasing the brain's endorphins and enkephalins, thereby mimicking the effects of morphine."*

The Biology of Hope

Jerome Groopman

Dr. Jerome Groopman is the chief of experimental medicine at Beth Israel Deaconess Medical Center in Boston. His research focuses on the basic mechanisms of blood disease, cancer, and AIDS. The following viewpoint is an excerpt from his book, The Anatomy of Hope. *It discusses the measurable, physiological changes that occur when patients believe they are receiving a particular treatment. The "placebo effect" does not occur because people imagine they are getting better or react less intensely to a disease stimulus; the placebo effect triggers a series of biochemical events that actually influence recovery.*

As you read, consider the following questions:

1. How do opiate drugs, like morphine, chemically work to block pain?

2. How does researcher Fabrizio Benedetti explain how the placebo effect affects subjects who believe they have been injected with morphine?

3. What role do doctors, nurses, and other medical authorities play in triggering the placebo effect?

To understand the experiments on placebos and pain, we need to know about the genesis of pain. Imagine a stubbed toe or a knife cut on a finger. Specific nerves in the tissues carry signals of pain to a part of the spinal cord called the "dorsal horn." The pain signal leaves the dorsal horn, the receiving area, and ascends the spinal cord at several points, as one runner in a relay race passes the baton on to the next. The finish line is in the brain, where we consciously perceive the pain.

Within the spinal and brain cord are cells that can turn pain signals on or off. They are aptly termed "on" and "off" cells. On cells increase pain and appear critical in withdrawal reflexes: The output of the on cells causes us to pull our hand off a hot burner or jerk away from the edge of a sharp knife, even before we consciously sense the pain. The off cells act like circuit breakers: They interrupt the flow of painful signals. If off cells were dominant, then we would not be primed for pain; rather, we would move numbly through the world, as if encased in armor. This would be a dangerous state, given that pain protects us from potentially damaging activities. So the on cells normally dominate and restrain the off cells, and we are wired to perceive pain—and to pull our hand off the burner or away from the knife.

Certain powerful drugs derived from the opium poppy, like morphine, can block pain. They work by throwing up roadblocks in the central nervous system and, in effect, stopping the relay runner from passing on the baton. An injection of morphine works by shutting down the on cells. When on cells are shut down by opiates, the off cells are free to block the flow of painful signals. For a while, our neural circuits are switched off, and we function as if we were indeed wearing a suit of armor.

What does this have to do with hope? It turns out that we have our own natural forms of morphine—within our brains are chemicals akin to opiates. These chemicals are called "endorphins" and "enkephalins." Belief and expectation, cardinal components of hope, can block pain by releasing the brain's endorphins and enkephalins, thereby mimicking the effects of morphine. This conclusion has been substantiated by several research groups. One of the leaders in the field is Dr. Fabrizio Benedetti, of the Department of Neuroscience at the University of Turin in Italy.

A classical Benedetti experiment involves a research assistant causing a volunteer pain by compressing a cuff around the arm, in effect cutting off circulation with viselike pressure. The volunteer, a young man, winces in response. He is attached by recording wires to a series of monitors that document physiological changes in response to the painful stimulus. With the pressure, there is increased heart rate, sweating, blood pressure, and muscle contraction. It takes a few moments for the tension in the volunteer's face and limbs to pass when the cuff is deflated.

The research assistant wears a spotless starched white coat and tells the volunteer in an authoritative voice that prior to the next stimulus, an injection of morphine will be given to prevent any pain. A syringe from the researcher's pocket appears. The volunteer's eyes follow the assistant as he picks up the vial of morphine and fills the syringe. The drug is injected. A few minutes are allowed to elapse before the cuff is once again inflated. The volunteer does not wince or otherwise react. The recording devices show no changes in heart rate, sweating, blood pressure, or muscle contraction. Pretreated with morphine, the volunteer feels no pain.

The procedure is repeated several times in sequence, the syringe filled, the morphine injected, the painful stimulus given, with the same outcome: The volunteer feels no pain. The wariness that marked the volunteer's eyes when he sat down in the lab and was hooked up to the monitors is gone. Rather, his mien is relaxed.

Then the researcher again holds up a syringe, fills it with a clear fluid from a glass vial, and authoritatively tells the volunteer that the injection will be administered. But this time the vial contains saline, which is essentially table salt dissolved in water.

The cuff is inflated. But the volunteer shows no signs of distress or discomfort. The recordings on the monitors do not jump: The heart rate is steady, blood pressure normal, skin cool and dry, muscles relaxed. The research assistant asks the volunteer how he feels. He reports no pain. None? the assistant asks. No, none whatsoever.

How can this be, that a placebo like saline can mimic morphine?

Benedetti's hyphothesis is that the volunteer's belief and expectation that he is receiving a potent drug like morphine generates signals in his brain that release his endorphins and enkephalins. These chemicals course through the spinal fluid and bathe the pain circuits, shutting off the on cells, restraining the runners that pass on the baton of pain. With his on cells blocked, the volunteer's off cells snap into action. The off cells throw up their barriers along the pain pathways. The messages of pain from the nerve fibers on his skin where the stimulus was given are not transmitted. They are stopped cold when they enter the first way station in the spinal cord. His brain never receives them.

Benedetti proves his hypothesis in another experiment that again uses a sleight of hand. The researcher again gives the volunteer a painful stimulus, with the expected painful response. Again he tells the volunteer that a powerful painkiller

The Nocebo Effect: Placebo's Evil Twin

The word nocebo, Latin for "I will harm," doesn't represent a new idea—just one that hasn't caught on widely among clinicians and scientists. More than four decades after researchers coined the term, only a few medical journal articles mention it. Outside the medical community, being "scared to death" or "worried sick" are expressions that have long been part of the popular lexicon, noted epidemiologist Robert Hahn from the Centers for Disease Control and Prevention in Atlanta.

Is such language just hyperbole? Not to those who accept, for example, the idea of voodoo death—a hex so powerful that the victim of the curse dies of fright. While many in the scientific community may regard voodoo with skepticism, the idea that gut reactions may have biological consequences can't be simply dismissed.

"Surgeons are wary of people who are convinced that they will die," said Herbert Benson, a Harvard professor and the president of Mind/Body Medical Institute in Boston. "There are examples of studies done on people undergoing surgery who almost want to die to re-contact a loved one. Close to 100 percent of people under those circumstances die."

Brian Reid, "The Nocebo Effect: Placebos Evil Twin,"
The Washington Post, *April 30, 2002.*

will be administered before the next cuff pressure. Morphine is given, and pain is blocked; this sequence is repeated several times. Then the second sleight of hand occurs. With the next cuff pressure, the researcher fills the syringe with neither morphine nor saline but Naloxone, a drug that blocks the receptors for endorphins and enkephalins in the brain. Naloxone is like an obnoxious bus passenger who not only occupies his seat but spreads out on all the seats around him. There is no place for anyone else to sit down. That is, Naloxone sits on the surface receptors of the brain's on cells, so there are no "seats" available for the endorphins or enkephalins. These cerebral chemicals are still released but cannot dampen the pain pathways, since their receptors are occupied by Naloxone.

Although the volunteer expects that he is being injected with morphine, he shows the effects of pain: His heart beats quickly, his palms grow moist, his blood pressure rises. Naloxone prevents the placebo effect. Although endorphins and enkephalins are released by belief and expectation, they fail to block the pain signals because Naloxone interferes with their contacting the nerve cells.

There are other chemicals in the central nervous system that can modulate pain circuits, amplifying pain. Substance P is one of them, and another is cholecystokinin, or CCK. It appears that CCK works in part by blocking endorphins and thus enhancing pain. Some researchers contend that expectation and belief also interfere with CCK release, thereby enhancing the analgesic effects of endorphins and enkephalins.

Scientists studying the experimental scenario above try to enter the mind of the volunteer and categorize his psychological responses into functional parts. Each visual, auditory, and tactile component in the experiment and in the behavior of the researcher is a cue, perceived and processed by the volunteer. The starched white coat, authoritative voice, statements about the drugs, and deployment of the syringe are all cues that affect the mind-set of the volunteer. The two major changes are belief and expectation: The volunteer *believes* and *expects* that he will receive pain from the cuff and comfort from the morphine. He also *desires* to avoid pain. Belief, expectation, and desire activate brain circuits that cause the release of endorphins and enkephalins, and perhaps the inhibition of CCK.

Dr. Ted Kaptchuk, who studies placebos at Harvard Medical School, sees the environmental cues and the behavior of an authority figure as part of the ritual of medicine that dates to ancient shamans. And, he emphasizes, a change in mind-set can alter neurochemistry, both in a laboratory setting and in the clinic. When we are patients, suffering from pain and debility, we look to our doctors and nurses for the words and gestures that reinforce our belief in medicine's power and solidify our expectation that we may benefit from an intervention. Recent research shows just how catalytic those neurochemical changes can be in the course of certain maladies.

Periodical Bibliography

The following articles have been selected to supplement the diverse views presented in this chapter.

Christopher M. Bache — "Reincarnation and the Akashic Field: A Dialogue with Ervin Lazlo," *World Futures*, January–March 2006.

S.K. Bardwell — "Man Shows Others How to 'Hear' Voices: Smith, Students Pursue Mysterious Electronic Voice Phenomena," *Houston Chronicle*, August 31, 2006.

Sandra Blakeslee — "Out-of-Body Experience? Your Brain Is to Blame," *New York Times*, October 3, 2006.

Ellen Goldberg — "Cognitive Science and Hathayoga," *Zygon*, September 2005.

John Hegelin — "The Power of the Collective," *Shift*, June–August, 2007.

Craig M. Klugman — "Dead Men Talking: Evidence of Post-Death Contact and Continuing Bonds," *Omega: The Journal of Death and Dying*, November 2006.

Steven Kotler — "Extreme States: Out-of-Body Experiences? Near-Death Experiences? Researchers Are Beginning to Understand How They Occur and How They May Alter the Brain," *Discover*, July 2005.

Mary Roach — "What Happens after You Die? We Have All Wondered if There Is an Afterlife, but Only a Few Are Brave—or Foolish—Enough to Try and Find Out," *New Scientist*, November 18, 2006.

Kim Underwood — "Love's Déjà vu: Visions, Reincarnation Led to Second Marriage 125 Years Later," *Winston-Salem Journal*, May 24, 2007.

Tim Vasquez — "Another Tall Tale? Weather Records Question the Truth Behind the Amityville Horror," *Weatherwise*, September–October 2006.

Should Government Support the Paranormal?

Chapter Preface

The separation of church and state is one of the most cherished elements of the Constitution of the United States. The provision protects religious citizens and nonreligious citizens alike: government does not dictate to religious citizens how they should practice their faiths, so they are free to worship as they choose; government does not dictate to nonreligious citizens that they should practice any faith, so they are free to abstain as they choose. The reality is, of course, much more complicated than the ideal, but the mere fact that cases involving the separation of church and state appear in court so often demonstrates that it is a vibrant and relevant principle. Belief is a sacred freedom as well as a very personal one—too personal to thrust upon someone else without their permission. It is a private matter.

A trickier enterprise is the balance of belief and disbelief in paranormal phenomena. In this debate, one person's truth is often another person's nonsense, and the line between them is often quite blurry. Skeptics discredit phenomena as fantasy or wishful thinking; believers in the phenomena point out that the history of science is full of radical discoveries that overturn traditional theories. This disparity of thought is not necessarily a source of conflict; a skeptic and a believer could live quite happily on the same street. Does it really hurt the skeptic if the believer wears magnetic jewelry to facilitate the healing energy of the body? Does it really hurt the believer if the skeptic has no hope of enjoying life after death?

Problems between the two groups arise on the national level, however, because of the government's support (or neglect) of paranormal research—usually monetary. Money is frequently given to scientists to conduct experiments in order to increase the body of knowledge that improves the quality of life. Public money is provided by tax-paying citizens; citizens work hard to earn what money they have and they do not want it spent frivolously. Rarely do people object when their money is spent on "noble" causes, like the study of new treatments to help prematurely born babies. People do object, though, when government spends money on projects that they consider pointless or wasteful, like the establishment of an indoor rainforest in Iowa. They also object when government underfunds something they think is important, like public education or alternative sources of energy.

Believers and nonbelievers of paranormal phenomena do not agree on what is considered paranormal. Unlike religion, in which there is either a deity or there is not, "paranormal phenomena" is a broad term that describes concepts ranging from the plausible to the fantastic. The practice of Eastern medicine, for example, includes treatments that can be described as paranormal; should the government "waste money" by funding research or "stifle research" in a promising field by cutting off funding? Both strategies will anger one taxpayer or another. Believers in the efficacy of Eastern medicine present data and experimental results to support their claims; skeptics of the efficacy of Eastern medicine dispute the researchers' methodology or present their own data to debunk the claims. As the two camps argue, the government makes another decision about hiring a dowser to locate groundwater, or including a session on connecting to the cosmos in the next human resources training event.

The following chapter explores the types of conflicts that arise when personal belief in the paranormal becomes a public rather than a private issue.

> "If a psychic offers free information to us over the phone, we will listen to them politely, but we do not take them seriously. It is a waste of time."

Psychic Detectives Hamper Police Investigations

Bret Christian

Bret Christian is the editor and proprietor of a newspaper group in Perth, Australia. He has been in journalism for more than twenty-five years; his newspapers specialize in local issues that affect individuals. The following viewpoint reports that police departments are besieged with unhelpful hints from bogus psychics (although not necessarily fraudulent ones); the time departments spend just managing the unusable information takes away from time they could use to locate missing people and murderers. In fact, police departments worldwide dismiss claims that psychic detectives are helpful.

As you read, consider the following questions:

1. Why did the skeptical Don Spiers follow up on the leads given to him by psychics regarding his daughter's disappearance?

Bret Christian, "Murders and Clairvoyants," The *Skeptic* (Australia), Autumn 2004, pp. 6–8. Reproduced by permission.

2. How did the psychic investigation by Gerard Croiset disrupt an entire community?

3. What tends to be the reaction of police departments and other investigative organizations to psychic detectives?

Skeptics sometimes find amusing the bizarre claims of clairvoyants, but there are many instances when their antics add to the trauma and heartache of bereaved people. Human tragedy is a fertile ground for clairvoyants, striking relatives and friends at their most vulnerable. Unthinking clairvoyants who offer unsolicited "visions" that add immeasurably to grief at this time are singularly unfunny.

Family Tragedies

Of all human loss, the most difficult for any parent to imagine is the shattering sadness of losing a child. On Australia day 1996, Sarah Spiers, a secretary aged 18, went with friends to a nightclub in the business district of Claremont, a well-to-do suburb halfway between Perth and Fremantle in Western Australia. She knew the area well, having spent her schooldays in an adjoining suburb. Sarah left the club at about 2am and walked to the next street, where phone records show she called a taxi. When the cab arrived [there] was no sign of her. She has never been seen since.

Initially, police treated her disappearance as a missing person, perhaps a runaway. But her family knew this was not possible. She would never fail to communicate with her loving family, under any circumstances. Sarah had shared a unit with her sister and there was nothing in her background to indicate that she would voluntarily vanish. Her distraught parents searched for Sarah, printing posters and making public pleas for anyone holding her to return her safely.

Just four months later, Jane Rimmer, a 23 year old child care worker who had been to another Claremont nightspot, vanished in the early hours of the morning. Her body was found in bush 40 kilometres south of Perth. Police believed she had been killed within hours of her abduction. Panic set in when 27 year old lawyer Ciara Glennon vanished nine months later from the same strip around midnight. A serial killer was at large, the police said, and would strike again.

All this time Don and Carol Spiers had not given up hope of finding Sarah alive. Don Spiers took time off from the shearing team he ran, and the couple moved into their daughters' city apartment. They publicised the phone number in the hope that anyone with information would come forward, and made sure at least one family member was by the phone 24 hours a day.

They got plenty of information, but it was bad information. It came in a torrent from the fevered minds of clairvoyants, around 250 of them. The callers told the desperate Spiers parents of dreams and visions that would lead them to their daughter. The calls placed Don Spiers into an agonising and cruel dilemma. He did not believe in clairvoyants but was compelled to do everything in his power to find Sarah. He felt he had to act on the information because he was concerned that one of the callers might have some factual information to offer but was hiding behind the persona of a clairvoyant.

'*They have been a huge torment to myself and my family in giving cryptic clues as to where Sarah might be,*' he told the ABC's *Australian Story* in February.

Psychic Clues Aren't Helpful

Many of the clues sounded specific, but they were just not specific enough. One clairvoyant told of a house in the inner Perth suburb of Wembley where Sarah was being held against her will. The seer described a house that was in a treelined street, with a white picket fence and a For Sale sign at the front. But the vision mysteriously did not include a street name or house number.

Every street in Wembley has street trees. Don Spiers spent hours driving the streets looking for the right house, without success. On another occasion he made the long, sad car trip alone to the old gold mining town of Southern Cross, 250 km east of Perth, where he was to find a man fitting a certain description in a pub. This man held the key. But again he drove home empty handed, frustrated, angry and shattered.

He described a night spent at an isolated reach of Perth's Canning River. "I remember one night, early days, I was down Salters Point, thrashing around in the swampy areas down there at 11 o'clock at night. . . walking around, bawling my eyes out and getting nowhere".

What Motivates Psychics?

A frustrating aspect of this sorry saga is that the callers to the Spiers family were almost certainly acting without malice. They were "only trying to help". A dream or a thought had popped into their heads and they thought the "information" should be passed on. Just why did they give credence to these visions? What were the thought processes that led them to pick up the phone to call a grieving family of strangers when they had nothing of value to offer?

One can only speculate on the influence of trashy television programs and magazine features that give psychics undeserved credibility. The producers of these programs sacrifice truth for ratings and advertising dollars by sucking in gullible viewers. They don't want to spoil the effect by putting the sceptical viewpoint, by pointing out that no-one has ever demonstrated the ability to "see" the unseeable or communicate with the dead. Perhaps these exploitive programs should be required to carry a warning that they are simply magician shows, for entertainment only.

Influencing the psychics who pedalled heartache and grief to the Spiers family may have been the long history of con-men and women who have been given prominence in the news media by claiming to have helped police solve serious crimes, usually murder, a guarantee for headlines.

Croiset and the Beaumont Case

There are many such examples, the most infamous in Australia being the Dutch clairvoyant Gerard Croiset. The horrifying missing persons story that Croiset bought into is still seared into the minds of any Australian old enough to remember as far back as 1966. On Australia Day (the type of coincidence much loved by psychics) two girls, Jane, 9, Arnna, 7, and their young brother Grant, 4, disappeared from Glenelg Beach near Adelaide after a morning of swimming and playing on the beach with a "tall, blond man." No trace of them has ever been found.

Their stricken parents raised the alarm, and a massive search was mounted. The usual crop of clairvoyants with "information" gleaned from dreams, séances and psychic visions bothered the Adelaide police. The followers of Croiset, a self-proclaimed psychic, hired a helicopter to take photographs of the beachfront which were sent to him in Holland, along with press cuttings, prints and other information. Croiset relayed the results of his ever-changing visions back to Adelaide.

His followers dug all over the place—in sandhills, in a blocked drainpipe and in the yard of a children's institution, where a bulldozer was hired to shift tonnes of sand. Skeptics will be unsurprised to learn that nothing was found.

A Psychic Circus

These false hopes added immeasurably to the anxiety and grief of Grant and Nancy Beaumont. All their children had vanished and the psychics were offering false hope as to their location. But failure was not to deter Croiset. In 1967 he travelled to Adelaide, arriving to a celebrity welcome, and the charade continued. He declared himself certain as to the location of the buried children, and armed with a sketch-pad, camera

A Grieving Father Speaks Against Psychic Detectives

[Psychic detectives] scan the media for the haunting eyes of desperate parents willing to do anything to recover their children and then they show up on your doorstep, literally or figuratively, to make the pitch. They claim to be on the cutting edge of communications, able to predict future events and reach into heaven and hell with their mind. They hold your hand, massage your psyche and convince you that the only thing separating you from their extraordinary gift is your money. . . .

Psychic detectives do not possess supernatural insight, they do not converse with the missing or the dead, they never bring children home.

Klaas Kids Foundation, "Hazards," 2002.
www.klaaskids.org.

and tape-recorder, set off with his acolytes in pursuit. After two days and a whole series of ever-changing locations, he failed to produce anything.

He then dramatically changed his mind again and declared that the children were buried under new food warehouse that had just been built. The South Australian government resisted strong public pressure to spend $7000 replacing the floor of the warehouse, but a committee of citizens raised the money. A wall of the factory was knocked down and the floor dug up. Nothing was found. Business was disrupted, thousands of dollars were wasted and false hopes were shattered.

But that, sadly was not the end of it. In 1996, 16 years after Gerard Croiset's death, followers of the discredited clairvoyant had another go. At great cost they decided to re-excavate the warehouse site again. Again, no trace of the missing children was found.

Police Responses to Psychic Claims

So-called psychic detectives who allegedly help police solve crimes have been a thriving industry in the United States, their reputations booming after appearances on television talk shows, their claims unquestioned by the hosts. But even in California, the spiritual home of the way-out, the police dismiss such claims.

The Los Angeles Police Department issued this statement:

The LAPD has not, does not and will not use psychics in the investigation of crimes, period.

If a psychic offers free information to us over the phone, we will listen to them politely, but we do not take them seriously. It is a waste of time.

A study into the subject by the LAPD's behavioural science services and police psychologist concluded that the hit rate of psychic detectives was statistically no better than chance. The department's public relations department says:

It is important to note that no information that would have been investigatively useful, such as first and last names, licence plate numbers, apartment house locations etc. was accurately produced by any of the subjects.

The UK's Scotland Yard has the same policy. The Yard's Inspector Edward Ellidon stated:

Scotland Yard never approaches psychics for information. There are no official police psychics in England.

The Yard does not endorse psychics in any way.

There is no recorded instance in England of any psychic solving a criminal case or providing evidence or information that led directly to its solution.

Deliberately Fraudulent?

The dramatic claims made by psychics to have "seen" vital clues often fall into the category of retrospective predictions. They are only slightly more sophisticated versions of: "I dreamed about the Melbourne Cup winner—I should have backed it."

Writes Kelly Roberts in *Psychic Investigations: A Clairvoyant's Diary of Assisting Law Enforcement*: "Did he tie her up?" I asked (the police) . . . did he tie her up with shoe laces?

"They all looked at me, then at one another . . . they seemed surprised that I knew."

This kind of self-serving tripe can easily tip over into blatant fraud of the kind exposed by Harry Houdini.

There is another category of eerily accurate psychic detective work described by leading US skeptic James Randi.

A man claiming to be a psychic attracted the interest of police when he predicted a serious industrial fire. The accuracy of the detail after the event could only have been provided by the psychic's special powers. But police discovered that he had no need of paranormal powers to produce his visions—he himself was the arsonist.

It was the prospect of just such a claim that led Sarah Spiers' family to sit by the phone to face the agonising prospect of one more misguided psychic call.

> *"Parapsychology uses the methodology of science to study aspects of the human experience which seem to fall outside our present knowledge base."*

The Study of Paranormal Phenomena Is Legitimate Science

Scott Flagg

Author Scott Flagg is a researcher in the fields of counseling and consciousness studies, including field research related to human experiences of the extraordinary. The following viewpoint is a response to the "Parapsychology" entry in the Skeptic's Dictionary *by Robert Carroll. The dictionary article assesses paranormal research as unscientific in scope and methodology; Flagg acknowledges that some paranormal investigators do not perform sound experiments but argues that paranormal research can be scientific and in fact provides information that can explain scientific mysteries and identify new fields of study.*

As you read, consider the following questions:

1. According to Flagg, why did the study of parapsychology originate?

Scott Flagg, "Response to Robert T. Carroll," *American Institute of Parapsychology* (www.parapsychologylab.com), 2007. Reproduced by permission.

2. How does the author address past flaws in parapsychology research?

3. Why doesn't Flagg consider the lack of a scientific framework for understanding PSI phenomena to be a problem?

It is absurd to say that parapsychology is a non-scientific study or more specifically that *it* is biased towards a specific outcome. This statement originates in [Robert Carroll's] false assumptions that all such phenomena can be explained by known physical and psychological processes. Parapsychology uses the methodology of science to study specific aspects of the human experience which seem to fall outside our present knowledge base. The operative word here is "study," not "search" or "presume." Parapsychology did not originate to prove the existence of superstitious belief or magical thinking. It originated because people *do* experience events which they themselves describe as: transformative, transpersonal, extraordinary and exceptional. As with all sciences, personal bias is often interjected into research. While there are faculty parapsychologists who have presumed events to be of supernatural origin there are also, as illustrated here, debunkers who assume that consciousness and reality are "solved" functions. . . .

Moving Beyond Past Shortcomings

Parapsychological research in recent years has become adept at minimizing external influences and confounding variables in both psychokinetic and probability studies. Well-performed studies are self-correcting and take into account relevant natural causes. Call the phenomena what you will: parapsychologists use the term PSI which is a general term implying that consciousness interacts with materiality in some as of yet unknown manner. Describing data in this way is an assumption and may ultimately prove untrue. However, due to the sophistication and outcome of such studies it is inadequate to say

Course Description for States of Consciousness and Parapsychology

The Center for Research on Consciousness and Anomalous Psychology (CERCAP) in the Department of Psychology is currently inviting applicants to pursue a PhD in Psychology. . . . CERCAP will be focusing on the following areas of research in the next few years:

1. Potential research areas include: the development of a taxonomy of these and other (e.g., OBEs) anomalous experiences including germane psychological characteristics (e.g., schizotypy, dissociativity); the examination of the necessary and sufficient conditions (psychology, biological, social, and environmental) for the presence of anomalous experiences; and the development of a theoretical account of anomalous experiences which is phenolmenologically, biologically, and culturally informed. . . .

2. Researching the relationship between hypnotizability and performance in controlled psi (parapsychological) experiments. . . .

3. Examining the nature of hypnotizability by assessing its characteristics and developmental pathways. . . .

Doctoral students are expected to focus their dissertation work (75–100%) on one or more of these areas, but queries regarding germane topics are welcomed.

Source: Etzel Cardeña,
"States of Consciousness and Parapsychology"
Doctoral Study Invitation, March 2007.

parapsychologists' assumptions are unfounded or unreasonable. Another way of looking at this topic is to ask why the debunker assumes such data to be of known mechanism when no such factors appear to adequately explain the phenomena.

Debunkers could participate scientifically if, rather than generally saying parapsychologists assume too much, they offered an explanation which properly accounts for the phenomena. . . .

I believe it to be fair and relevant to say that parapsychology has a tainted past. Many well-studied and fair-minded people have been deceived with beliefs of the supernatural and unexplainable. I see no good reason however to single out parapsychology as being flawed. Every branch of science has its scandals and misconceptions. What is relevant is that substantive review and suspensions of belief systems occur in the practice of all research. The bottom line is that there are still a large number of human experiences which are yet unexplained. Science should not shun or exhibit bias towards such experiences because they defy our current conceptual framework. . . .

Close-Minded Criticism

While it is true that some parapsychologists falsely identify natural phenomena as PSI there is a large body of evidence in support of PSI. Overall there is certainly enough evidence that further research is warranted. It simply isn't science if you throw out evidence because it defies what is expected. . . .

> Parapsychologists who claim to have found positive results often systematically ignore or rationalize their own studies if they don't support psi. Rhine discarded data that didn't support his beliefs, claiming subjects were intentionally getting answers wrong. Many, if not most, psi researchers allow optional starting and optional stopping. Most psi researchers limit their research to investigation parlor tricks (guessing the number of suit of a playing card, or "guess what Zener card I am looking at" or "try to influence this random number generator with your thoughts"). Any statistical strangeness is attributed to paranormal events.

The author [Carroll] refers to "statistical strangeness" without any explanation of what its cause is. None of the items above alter the statistical significance of a well-designed study. Again it isn't rational to accuse *all* parapsychologists as being fatally biased while at the same time taking such a polarized position. There have been a number of well done meta-analyses on the so-called "file drawer" or "trash can" effect. The results of studies such as Dean Radin's indicate that there is still a significant effect size with modern PSI studies. . . .

Expanding the Boundaries of Science

There is presently no predictable framework for discussing PSI. ESP experiments (and some physics experiments) do seem to indicate information transfer faster than light and that space/time as we know it as being only partially understood. Science allows us to expand our perspective of the world so long as we don't falsely cling to old views. It is a valid argument against PSI that there exists no conceptual model to which it might be compared. It should however be noted that compared to some presently accepted models in quantum physics, parapsychology studies seem middle of the road. . . .

Look at the studies yourself. Draw your own conclusions rather than believing blatantly biased opinions. Most modern researchers go to extraordinary lengths to try and account for confounding variables. It is important to understand that our view of the world and consciousness is incomplete. I have always viewed parapsychology as a field which is free to study the fringe phenomena that may provide the missing links so prevalent in other areas of study. Skepticism and curiosity are critical aspects of science. Personally I find the position of CSICOP [Committee for the Scientific Investigation of Claims of the Paranormal], and SKEPDIC [Skeptic's Dictionary] to be as polarized as that of many "True Believers" and religious fanatics. Science operates best when we are skeptically open to alternatives, not when we have already made up our minds and are simply trying to validate either our positive or negative beliefs.

"Accrediting a school for a technique which has no demonstrable basis in fact seems to be the very opposite of what accreditation should be about."

The Study of Paranormal Phenomena Is Not Legitimate Science

Barry Karr

Barry Karr is the executive director of the Committee for Skeptical Inquiry, an organization dedicated to the scientific investigation of paranormal claims and the dissemination of factual information to the public. The following viewpoint is a press release from Karr's office decrying the academic accreditation of the Astrological Institute, a school of higher education that offers formal degrees. Students attending accredited schools are eligible to receive federal financial aid and grants. The viewpoint laments that astrology has been given the same academic status as other disciplines of science—experiment-driven research characterized by peer review and reproducible results.

Barry Karr, "Accreditation Commission Approves Astrology School," *Committee for Skeptical Inquiry*, August 30, 2001. Copyright © 2001 Committee for the Scientific Investigation of Claims of the Paranormal (CSICOP). Reproduced by permission.

As you read, consider the following questions:

1. What is the basis of astrology as it will be taught at the Astrological Institute?

2. On what grounds did the Council for Higher Education Accreditation grant accreditation to the Astrological Institute?

3. How does founder Joyce Jensen justify the accreditation of an astrology program?

Is the Astrological Institute in Scottsdale, Arizona, a Leo or a Virgo? The school received its new nationwide accreditation from the Accrediting Commission of Career Schools and Colleges of Technology (ACCSCT) earlier this month [August 2001]—an apparent first in astrology. The institute's founder, Joyce Jensen, is elated; science organizations like the Committee for the Scientific Investigation of Claims of the Paranormal(CSICOP), however, see the recognition as a blow to the integrity of higher education.

The Astrological Institute offers full degrees in this ancient Babylonian art of divination, which is based on the premise that the positions of stars and planets affect people's personalities and fates. Belief in the practice persists despite the lack of any reliable scientific evidence that it actually works, according to Andrew Fraknoi, who is a CSICOP fellow and chair of the astronomy department at Foothill College in Los Altos Hills, California. "Although astrologers like to pretend such evidence does exist," says Fraknoi, "astrology has in fact been tested in dozens of excellent scientific trials, and it has consistently failed them. There's simply no evidence that astrology works—that it predicts anything or categorizes people in any way that can be used to help them."

Commenting on the Astrological Institute's accreditation in a recent Associated Press story, Judith Eaton, who heads the Council for Higher Education Accreditation in Washington,

U.S. Government Spends $400,000 on Dowsing

In January 2000, several Environmental Management field sites began conducting tests of Passive Magnetic Resonance Anomaly Mapping (PMRAM). PMRAM is a non-intrusive characterization technology that attempts to map the underground location of groundwater, faults, fractures, buried objects, and chemicals. This technology is unique in that it combines an electronic system and a human operator into a single bio-sensory unit by connecting the operator at the wrists to an electronic system, which is harnessed to the body. The technology relies on the ability of the world's only qualified operator, a resident of the Ukraine, to sense changes in magnetic fields.

The objective of the audit was to determine whether the OST [Office of Science and Technology] evaluated the technical merit and plausibility of PMRAM technology before field tests began.

RESULTS OF AUDIT

The Department spent over $400,000 to field test PMRAM prior to any OST evaluation of the merits and plausibility of the technology. In fact, OST was not even aware that field tests of the PMRAM technology had been conducted until Fiscal Year (FY) 2001.

In FY 2001, OST funding was requested to continue testing PM-RAM at other Environmental Management field locations. Once funding was requested, OST performed a peer review of the PMRAM technology. The peer review concluded that the technology:

- appeared to be implausible;

- did not allow for a scientifically based evaluation:

- provided no useful information during the three field demonstrations; and,

- appeared inadequate as a site-characterization tool.

We concluded that, had a peer review been performed prior to testing, the Department could have avoided spending over $400,000 on this technology.

Gregory Friedman,
Memo to the Secretary of the U.S. Department of Energy,
January 11, 2002.

DC, said that the accreditation does not validate astrology, but only recognizes, that the school fulfills its promises to students.

Validating the Paranormal

Scientists like Dr. Fraknoi dispute Eaton's distinction between the validity of the subject taught and quality of service to students. "Accrediting a school for a technique which has no demonstrable basis in fact seems to be the very opposite of what accreditation should be about. The notion that accreditation 'only recognizes that the school fulfills what it promises its students' is patently absurd. If a school were to promise that it would teach techniques for flying by leaping off cliffs with no equipment, I doubt any accrediting agency would rush to give them official sanctions. There should be similar hesitation about accrediting a school of astrology, which cannot demonstrate the reality or efficacy of what it teaches."

In an August 28, 2001, interview with Robert Siegel, host of NPR's [National Public Radio] *All Things Considered*, Joyce Jensen stated her belief the accreditation does lend credibility to astrology. When Siegel asked how she thought it would do this, Jensen focused on the vocation, not the science: "Because, you know, we've gone through the same process that every other school has gone through. So we've proven our ability to provide a program where people can find employment." For Jensen the popular perception of astrology as a legitimate vocation trumps the question of scientific credibility.

The nationwide accreditation of the institute takes astrology out of the realm of evening workshops at the local high school and "entertainment" horoscopes. In practical terms, as Dr. Fraknoi fears, the recognition elevates the subject to the same level as any other program at any other college or university. Accreditation will open the doors to student financial aid and grants paid for by federal tax dollars. It will also professionalize a lucrative business where, according to Jensen, astrologers charge clients between $100 and $150 per visit. By seeking the stamp of approval for the teaching of a vocation, the Astrology Institute has deftly shifted the question away from the qualifications of astrology to the qualifications of the astrologer.

Periodical Bibliography

The following articles have been selected to supplement the diverse views presented in this chapter.

Anna Borzello — "Crackdown on Nigeria TV Miracles," *BBC News*, April 30, 2004.

Monica Cafferky — "The Psychic Spies," *Daily Mail (London)*, May 21, 2004.

"Communicating with Angels 101," — Reuters, August 14, 2007.

Mark Forbes — "Spy agency accused of black magic murder," *Brisbane Times*, August 17, 2007.

Jessica Fraser — "The Abraham Cherrix Cancer Story the Media Won't Print: Harry Hoxsey's Cancer Cures and the U.S. Government Campaign to Destroy Them," *NewsTarget.com*, August 3, 2006.

"It's Haunted! Please Get Us out of Here!" — *Ilford Recorder*, August 24, 2006.

Selina Lum — "Fengshui Defence Helps Couple Avoid Property Deal Tax," *Strait Times*, September 7, 2007.

Matthew Philips — "Belief Watch: Reincarnate," *Newsweek*, August 20, 2007.

Gary Posner — "'Court TV' Psychic Loses to Skeptic in Real Court," *Skeptical Inquirer*, July–August 2007.

Andrew Purveis — "Cruise Film Gets German OK," *Time*, September 17, 2007.

Jim Stratton — "'Celestial Drops' Failed on Canker," *Orlando Sentinel*, July 5, 2005.

Caroline Watt — "Parapsychology's Contribution to Psychology: A View from the Front Line," *Journal of Parapsychology*, Fall 2005.

For Further Discussion

Chapter 1: Why Do People Believe in Paranormal Phenomena?

1. Robert Matthews argues that scientists are so committed to their beliefs about the existence of the paranormal that they ignore evidence that supports it. Susan Blackmore also writes about how difficult it is for a person to abandon his or her beliefs about how the world works, although she claims that evidence of paranormal phenomena does not exist. Consider the reasons Blackmore gives for her disbelief. In what ways does she fit or defy Matthews' description of a close-minded or stubborn scientist?

2. Michael Dougherty describes a college course in skeptical thinking that he says reduces belief in the paranormal. Dean Hamer describes characteristics of the human brain that make it susceptible to having paranormal experiences. Can education change how the brain works? Are courses that teach people to be skeptical of paranormal claims sufficient to overcome a biological predisposition to believe in them?

3. Robert Kenny uses scientific evidence to support the idea that humans are able to communicate with each other beyond the five physical senses. Martin Plimmer and Brian King use anecdote and reasoning to support the idea that people place too much emphasis on coincidence. Which side makes the stronger case? Is a scientific argument always the most convincing one?

Chapter 2: Do Paranormal Phenomena Exist?

1. Lucian Dorneanu debunks popular representations of ghosts by judging them against the laws of physics. Peter Novak supports popular representations of ghosts by comparing them to psychological disorders. If one author is right, does that make the other author wrong? Does physics trump psychology as a scientific means for assessing the probability that ghosts exist?

2. Janet McDonald presents a list of all the ways a psychic failed to predict her future despite charging a nonrefundable fee. Doug Moe reports on the success a psychic had finding a lost dog. Does Moe present an objective or compelling story? Does his account of a successful psychic lend credence to claims about psychic ability? Do the negative emotions McDonald has about her experience taint her assessment of the psychic? Is she angry about psychics in general or just that she fell prey to a fraudulent one?

Chapter 3: Are the Mind and Body Separate Entities?

1. G.M. Woerlee describes the "classic" near-death experience as a byproduct of the brain shutting down. Pim van Lommel describes it as consciousness approaching another plane of existence. Both authors emphasize the similarities of near-death experiences as described by the people who survive them. From Woerlee's perspective, the similarities come from the fact that the brain shuts down from oxygen deprivation the same way for every person; Lommel suggests that all consciousness leaving the body goes to the same place. What other factors might contribute to the similarities of reported experiences across cultures and other social groupings? Is it more likely that people experience the same thing or that they later tell the same story about their experience?

2. Gary Schwartz and William Simon claim that the nature of spiritual mediumship is such that exposure to skepticism hampers a medium's ability to communicate with the dead. Ray Hyman attributes any success a medium has transmitting a message from a dead person to a living loved one can be credited to teachable "reading" skills and enthusiasm on the part of the living loved one. If the client of a medium is happy with the reading and the medium believes that he helped the client, does it matter if the medium does not actually communicate with the dead (as skeptics say)? In what ways could a client who receives comfort from the experience also be harmed?

3. Roger Dobson details how hypnosis can be used as a strategy to treat many diseases and conditions. Jerome Groopman explains that detectable biochemical processes are triggered when a patient believes in a treatment's effectiveness. Is the brain's ability to influence the body a paranormal phenomena or an example of a natural process that has not yet been "discovered" by science? Should the placebo effect be relied upon as a legitimate tool in the treatment of disease?

Chapter 4: Should Government Support the Paranormal?

1. Bret Christian profiles how psychics complicate investigative searches and cause more harm than good. Is there evidence that psychics have helped detectives solve crimes? Is the chance a psychic could solve even just one crime reason enough to justify a police department turning to psychics for help, even if it is documented that most of the information a psychic provides is unusable?

2. Scott Flagg argues that the researchers of paranormal phenomena are often legitimate scientists. Barry Karr penned a press release panning the accreditation of a school that issues higher degrees in astrology. Neither author men-

tions universities that train people to be priests and ministers of churches, even though matters of God and religion fall into spiritual categories. Is there a difference between issuing a degree in paranormal practices and issuing a degree in religious practices? How might each author answer this question? Is there a benefit to society if government uses tax dollars to help educate astrologers or church leaders?

Organizations to Contact

The editors have compiled the following list of organizations concerned with the issues debated in this book. The descriptions are derived from materials provided by the organizations. All have publications or information available for interested readers. The list was compiled on the date of publication of the present volume; the information provided here may change. Be aware that many organizations take several weeks or longer to respond to inquiries, so allow as much time as possible.

Association for the Scientific Studies of Consciousness (ASSC)
Web site: www.assc.caltech.edu

The ASSC promotes research within cognitive science, neuroscience, philosophy, and other relevant disciplines in the sciences and humanities, directed toward understanding the nature, function, and underlying mechanisms of consciousness. The organization coordinates an annual conference on aspects of the scientific study of consciousness and facilitates consciousness research with awards for new investigators. It currently hosts Eprints, a free Internet archive of member contributions to the study of consciousness.

The Atlantic Paranormal Society (TAPS)/Paramagazine
657 Quarry Street, No. 5, Fall River, MA 02723
(508) 675-6666 • fax: (508) 675-6560
Web site: www.tapsparamag.com

TAPS is an organization of professional investigators of the paranormal. Its members follow a strict code of ethics and do not charge for their services. The organization publishes *TAPS Paramagazine*, which features articles by the top experts in the fields of ghosts, cryptozoology, ufology, and spiritual beliefs. The magazine aims to present an objective view of the unknown and mysterious, report on investigations, and debunk hoaxes. TAPS and *Paramagazine* are affiliated with the personalities featured on the television program *Ghost Hunters.*

Committee for Skeptical Inquiry (CSI)
Box 703, Amherst, NY   14226
(716) 636-1425
e-mail: info@csicop.org
Web site: www.csicop.org

Formerly the Committee for the Scientific Investigation of Claims of the Paranormal (CSICOP), CSI encourages the critical investigation of paranormal and fringe-science claims from a responsible, scientific point of view and disseminates factual information about the results of such inquiries to the scientific community and the public. It also promotes science and scientific inquiry, critical thinking, science education, and the use of reason in examining important issues. The organization publishes the monthly journal, *Skeptical Inquiry.* It also provides a roster of skeptical organizations worldwide.

Division of Perceptual Studies/University of Virginia Health Systems
PO Box 800152, Charlottesville, VA   22908
(434) 924-2281

The main purpose of the Division of Perceptual Studies is the scientific empirical investigation of phenomena that suggest that currently accepted scientific assumptions and theories about the nature of mind or consciousness, and its relationship to matter, may be incomplete. Examples of such phenomena, sometimes labeled "paranormal," include various types of extrasensory perception (such as telepathy), apparitions and deathbed visions (sometimes referred to as after-death communications or ADCs), poltergeists, experiences of persons who come close to death and survive (usually called near-death experiences or NDEs), out-of-body experiences (OBEs), and claimed memories of previous lives.

Institute of Noetic Sciences (IONS)
101 San Antonio Road, Petaluma, CA   94952
(707) 775-3500 • fax: (707) 781-7420
e-mail: membership@noetic.org
Web site: www.noetic.org

IONS is a nonprofit membership organization that conducts and sponsors research into the potentials and powers of consciousness—including perceptions, beliefs, attention, intention, and intuition. The Institute explores phenomena that do not necessarily fit conventional scientific models, while maintaining a commitment to scientific rigor. It publishes the magazine *Shift* and hosts a free online database of articles, book reviews, and research.

International Association for Near-Death Studies (IANDS)
PO Box 502, East Windsor Hill, CT   06028-0502
(860) 882-1211 • fax: (860) 882-1212
Web site: www.iands.org

IANDS is the informational and networking center in the field of near-death studies, the first organization in the world devoted to exploring near-death and similar experiences. Members include people who have had near-death experiences and people who have not had them, medical professionals, and the general public. IANDS hosts about fifty support groups in North America and publishes the newsletter *Vital Signs* and the scholarly *Journal of Near-Death Experiences*.

James Randi Educational Foundation (JREF)
201 SE Twelfth Street, Fort Lauderdale, FL   33316-1815
(954) 467-1112 • fax: (954) 467-1660
e-mail: jref@randi.org
Web site: www.randi.org

The James Randi Educational Foundation is a not-for-profit organization founded in 1996. Its aim is to promote critical thinking by reaching out to the public and media with reliable information about the paranormal and supernatural ideas so widespread in society today. In addition to public and educational outreach programs, the Foundation supports and conducts research into paranormal claims through well-designed experiments utilizing the scientific method. It also maintains a legal defense fund to assist people who are being attacked as a result of their investigations and criticism of people who make paranormal claims. It offers a $1,000,000 prize to any person or persons who can demonstrate any psychic, supernatural, or paranormal ability of any kind under mutually agreed upon scientific conditions.

National Center for Complementary and Alternative Medicine (NCCAM)

9000 Rockville Pike, Bethesda, MD 20892
(888) 644-6226 • fax: (866) 464-3616
e-mail: info@mccam.nih.gov
Web site: http://nccam.nih.gov

NCCAM is the federal government's lead agency for scientific research on complementary and alternative medicine (CAM), and one of the organizations that comprise the National Institutes of Health. The mission of NCCAM is to explore complementary and alternative healing practices in the context of rigorous science, train complementary and alternative medicine researchers, and disseminate authoritative information to the public and professionals.

Parapsychology Foundation, Inc.

PO Box 1562, New York, NY 10021-0043
(212) 628-1550 • fax: (212) 628-1559
e-mail: info@parapsychology.org
Web site: www.parapsychology.org

The Parapsychology Foundation supports scientific and academic research into psychic phenomena, and provides professional resources and information to the academic and lay communities. The Foundation maintains a library and archives, awards research and scholarly incentive grants, and publishes the *International Journal of Parapsychology*, as well as other pamphlets, monographs, conference proceedings, and books devoted to psychical research and parapsychology.

Quackwatch

Chatham Crossing, Chapel Hill, NC 27517

(919) 533-6009

e-mail: sbinfo@quackwatch.org

Web site: www.quackwatch.org

Quackwatch, Inc. is a nonprofit corporation established to combat health-related frauds, myths, fads, fallacies, and misconduct. Quackwatch investigates questionable health claims, debunks pseudoscientific claims, and tries to improve the quality of health information on the Internet. The organization's Web site is a resource of information and links to other Web sites that provide in-depth information on specific medical and health topics.

The Skeptics Society

PO Box 338, Altadena, CA 91001

(626) 794-3119 • fax: (626) 794-1301

e-mail: skepticsociety@skeptic.com

Web site: www.skeptic.com

The Skeptics Society, directed by Dr. Michael Shermer, is a scientific and educational organization of scholars, scientists, historians, magicians, professors, and teachers, and anyone curious about controversial ideas, extraordinary claims, revolutionary ideas, and the promotion of science. It serves as an educational tool for those seeking clarification and viewpoints on controversial ideas and claims by engaging in scientific investigation and journalistic research to investigate claims made by scientists, historians, and controversial figures on a wide range of subjects. Its goal is to promote critical thinking and lifelong inquisitiveness in all individuals. It publishes *Skeptic* magazine.

Society for Scientific Exploration (SSE)
Department of Astronomy, University of Virginia
Charlottesville, VA   22904-4325
Web site: www.scientificexploration.org

The SSE is a multi-disciplinary professional organization of scientists and other scholars committed to the rigorous study of unusual and unexplained phenomena that cross traditional scientific boundaries and may be ignored or inadequately studied within mainstream science. Topics addressed in its journal, *Journal for Scientific Exploration*, and in its regular meetings range from real or apparent anomalies in well-established areas of science to paradoxical phenomena that belong to no established discipline. It also supports a Young Investigators program to provide information and resources pertaining to the scholarly study of anomalous phenomena and other frontier areas of science.

Bibliography of Books

Dan Agin
Junk Science: An Overdue Indictment of Government, Industry, and Faith Groups that Twist Science for Their Own Gain. New York: St. Martin's Press, 2007.

Rosemary Altea
Soul Signs. Emmaus, PA: Rodale, 2004.

Wendell Berry
Life Is a Miracle: An Essay Against Modern Superstition. Washington, DC: Counterpoint, 2000.

Roberta Bivens
Alternative Medicine?: A History. New York: Oxford University Press, 2007.

Gregg Braden
The Divine Matrix: Bridging Time, Space, Miracles and Belief Carlsbad, CA: Hay House, 2006.

John Brockman (Ed.)
Intelligent Thought: Science versus the Intelligent Design Movement. New York: Random House, 2006.

Maureen Caudill
Suddenly Psychic: A Skeptic's Journey. Charlottesville, VA: Hampton Roads Publishing, 2006.

Kartar Diamond
Feng Shui for Skeptics: Real Solutions without Superstition. Culver City, CA: Four Pillars Publishing, 2004.

Allison DuBois
Don't Kiss Them Goodbye. New York: Fireside, 2004.

Erik Durschmied   *Whores of the Devil: Witch-Hunts and Witch-Trials*. Gloucestershire, UK: Sutton Publishing, 2007.

Taner Edis   *Science and Nonbelief* Amherst, NY: Prometheus, 2007.

John Edward   *Crossing Over*. Carlsbad, CA: Hay House, 2004.

Judith Hawkins-Tillirson   *The Weiser Concise Guide to Herbal Magick*. San Francisco: Red Wheel/ Weiser, 2007.

Harry Houdini   *A Magician among the Spirits*. Anster- dam: Fredonia Books, 2002.

Lynne Kelly   *The Skeptic's Guide to the Paranor- mal*. New York: Thunder's Mouth Press, 2004.

Ray Kurzweil   *The Singularity Is Near: When Hu- mans Transcend Biology*. New York: Penguin, 2006.

John Lerma   *Into the Light: Stories about Angelic Visits, Visions of the Afterlife, and Other Pre-Death Experiences*. Franklin Lakes, NJ: New Page Books, 2007.

Sheila Lyon and Mark Sherman   *Palms Up!: A Handy Guide to 21st Century Palmistry*. New York: Berke- ley Publishing Group, 2005.

Edward F. Malkowski   *The Spiritual Technology of Ancient Egypt: Sacred Science and the Mystery of Consciousness*. Rochester, VT: Inner Traditions, 2007.

Lynne McTaggart — *The Field: The Quest for the Secret Force of the Universe.* New York: Harper Collins, 2002.

Joe Nickell — *Adventures in Paranormal Investigation.* Lexington, KY: University of Kentucky Press, 2007.

Kenneth R. Pelletier — *The Best Alternative Medicine.* New York: Fireside, 2002.

Jim Richardson and Allen Richardson — *Gonzo Science: Anomalies, Heresies, and Conspiracies.* New York: Paraview Press, 2004.

Carl Sagan — *The Demon-Haunted World: Science as a Candle in the Dark.* New York: Ballantine Books, 1997.

Gary E. Schwartz and William L. Simon — *The Energy Healing Experiments: Science Reveals Our Natural Power to Heal.* New York: Simon & Schuster, 2007.

Michael Shermer — *Science Friction: Where the Known Meets the Unknown.* New York: Holt, 2005.

Russell Targ — *Limitless Mind: A Guide to Remote Viewing and Transformation of Consciousness.* Novato, CA: New World Library, 2004.

Tyler Volk — *Gaia's Body: Toward a Physiology of Earth.* Cambridge: MIT Press, 2003.

Sylvia Hart
Wright

*When Spirits Come Calling: The
Open-Minded Skeptic's Guide to After-
Death Contacts.* Nevada City, CA:
Blue Dolphin Publishing, 2002.

Index